BOARD MEMBERS

Governing Roles and Responsibilities

W. Astor Kirk

University Press of America,® Inc.
Lanham · Boulder · New York · Toronto · Plymouth, UK

Copyright © 2007 by
University Press of America,® Inc.
4501 Forbes Boulevard
Suite 200
Lanham, Maryland 20706
UPA Acquisitions Department (301) 459-3366

Estover Road
Plymouth PL6 7PY
United Kingdom

Library of Congress Control Number: 2006937933
ISBN-13: 978-0-7618-3669-8 (paperback : alk. paper)
ISBN-10: 0-7618-3669-1 (paperback : alk. paper)

DEDICATION

To my four granddaughters—Ayanna Dunn, Jennele Lyons, Allison Kirk, and Stefanie Kirk—for their unbounded love and for the innumerable ways in which they have made the second half of my life so richly meaningful.

CONTENTS

LIST OF FIGURES, BOXES, AND EXHIBITS

FIGURES

BOXES

EXHIBITS

Preface

BOARD MEMBERS: Governing Roles and Responsibilities is a book that rests on the foundation of the following basic proposition: Certain types of collective activities, cognitive behaviors, and systems processes are generic to all functioning organizations.

Conceptually, I view these activities, behaviors and processes as **leading, guiding, directing** and **controlling.**

Early in the 1960s, I was appointed staff director of a church-government relations research project. The Board of Church and Society of the United Methodist Church, which is located in Washington, DC, sponsored the project. A primary goal of the project was broadening understanding of the diverse public policy settings in which issues of so-called 'separation of church and state' emerged from time to time. In working with that project, I soon discovered that the 1960s *social activism* of the federal government was spawning a very important and unique species of organizations. All of the new organizations were *nonprofits*—they had a legally defined not-for-profit (LDNFP) status.

I realized that although all of these emerging forms of organization had an LDNFP status, they did not fit neatly into what was then, and still is today, conventionally referred to as 'the nonprofit world' or 'the nonprofit sector,' or 'the voluntary sector.' They represent a very important subcategory of the large universe of organizations with the LDNFP status. Organizations that comprise this subcategory share five defining attributes. All of them:

- Have public-serving missions;
- Exist outside the formal structures of government;
- Have a wide range of relationships with government agencies;
- Are operated on a non-commercial basis; and

- Are incorporated entities.

This book had a long gestation period. It is actually a spin-off of an ongoing theoretical and academically oriented research project that I began in the mid-1980s. That project involves studying the governance and strategic management of certain types of organizations with the LDNFP status.

In November 1968, I was appointed director of the five-state (and District of Columbia) Mid-Atlantic Region of the U. S. Office of Economic Opportunity—the national anti-poverty agency of the federal government at that time. I made grants to many community action agencies (CAAs) and other new nontraditional entities with the LDNFP status. At the time, I conveniently referred to these entities as public-serving nongovernmental organizations (PSNOs).

Today, for the sake of both brevity and convenience, I refer to these entities as nongovernmental public-serving (**NPS**) organizations.1

In the NPS organization, the cybernetic behaviors of leading, guiding, directing and controlling occur in two domains. The first is a domain of *governance*; the second is a domain of *management.*

This book is about leading, guiding, directing and controlling behaviors within the institutional context of the NPS organization. Its focus is on *governance.*

---

1. There are, as yet, no generally recognized terms to describe the subcategory of entities that this book labels *NPS organizations.* Many metaphors have been used. For example, Pifer (1967) called them "quasi-nongovernmental organizations;" Scott Greer (1972) called them "parapolitical organizations;" Kenneth Boulding (1973) used the term "intersect organizations" to refer to them; Musolf and Seidman (1980) dubbed them "twilight-zone organizations." While not giving these entities a specific name, Weidenbaum (1969) viewed them as representing "the modern public sector;" Smith (1975) saw them as "the new political economy"; Schultze (1977) viewed them as examples of "the public use of private interest"; and Wolch (1990) conceptualizes them as a component of "the shadow state."

All of these writers and commentators seem to agree with Ansoff (1979, 8) that "The growing complexity of society's work and the changing social values have led to a recognition that historical organizational forms are no longer adequate for meeting society's needs. ...Thus it appears that the distinction between 'private for-profit' vs. 'public not-for-profit' is inadequate, either for explaining behavior or for designing new socially responsive forms."

This book is unique in that it does not treat the function of governance as it pertains to the entire category of not-for-profit organizations, which comprise 'the nonprofit sector.' Rather, the book focuses on the performance of governing roles within the institutional context of only a subcategory of organizations that is defined by five attributes. The attributes are described in the book's Introduction.

Organizational actors in the domain of governance exercise inherent and ultimate authority. Conversely, the actors in the domain of management exercise only delegated authority.

The book deals primarily with the domain of governance. It identifies and elaborates upon seven sets of roles and responsibilities of governing actors—i.e., members of governing bodies of NPS organizations.

A critical issue that concerns us in this book is the major societal purposes and functions, both actually and prescriptively, of NPS organizations. In the United States of America, these institutions impact the lives of millions of individuals in a multitude of diverse ways.

No less urgent, therefore, is the matter of how to get the men and women who occupy seats on governing boards to think long, hard and systematically about the fundamentals involved in leading, guiding, directing and controlling the affairs of NPS organizations.

Last but not least is our concern with the issue of how can governing board members ensure that the combined economic and non-economic transactions of NPS organizations produce sufficient operating revenues to keep them viable as invaluable institutional adjuncts of a radically changing welfare state.

On several occasions during the past two decades I have engaged in serious dialogue with individuals and groups who have sincerely asked such unsettling questions as

- "Why do NPS organizations have governing boards?"
- "Are governing boards really necessary?"
- "Is it true, as some literature suggests, that governing boards are a 'paradoxical' component of the NPS organization?"
- "Why can't the concept of governing boards be junked and leave running of NPS organizations entirely to 'professional' managers and their subordinate staffs?"

I have dealt with various aspects of these questions in the book's Introduction. A few comments about them here will give the reader a preliminary view of the institutional contexts in which such questions are nested.

First, there is an easy and simple answer to the question why NPS organizations must have governing boards. By definition, they are corporations. Some governmental agencies have granted them articles of incorporation. All states have laws that require some kind of governing board for corporations. So, in order to take advantage of the authority, power and privilege that corporate status confers on an entity, NPS organizations must have governing boards.

Second, a vital public trust is involved in the creation, existence and continual support of an NPS organization. Entities that have the five defining attributes of the NPS organization are integral components of local polities, whose public instrumentalities include more than governmental institutions (Elazar 1971, 4). Governing boards are necessary to create and sustain the legitimacy of NPS organizations, as institutions deserving of public trust.

Third, all human organizations are open, more or less adaptive social systems. They attempt in various ways to cope with the environment in which they exist. By definition, NPS organizations are not operated on a commercial basis. Therefore, they have to obtain substantial portions of their operating revenues from sources other than direct beneficiaries or users of their products and services. NPS organizations have to design and pursue effective resource-mobilization strategies in addition to their complex and non-economic transactions with the environment. It is probably unlikely that this task can be accomplished successfully over a long period of time without a functioning governing board.

Fourth, NPS organizations operate in highly pluralistic environments. The twentieth century gave us what Drucker (1969) described as "a new pluralism." In major urban areas, we have a very high degree of pluralism, not only demographically but also in the variety of societal institutions. A cybernetic system composed only of management would be totally inadequate for the typical NPS organization. That kind of cybernetic system could not successfully steer an NPS organization through the politics of institutional pluralism.

Fifth, and finally, the management component of NPS organizations, like its counterpart in the *business corporation*, needs an organ for review and advice. Governing boards provide executive managers with someone to talk to and a group that can review executive policies. Also, they monitor the performance of chief staff executives.

By focusing on the institutional context of NPS organizations, the book avoids a serious conceptual error, which is widely prevalent in the literature discussing 'nonprofit organizations.' It is the fact that particular principles, issues and problems are generally discussed as if they apply equally to all entities with the LDNFP status.

Thus, throughout the book I challenge a commonly held misconception about NPS enterprises. It is the popular notion that these enterprises are undifferentiated parts of the *nonprofit sector*. I recognize and acknowledge the reality that some very important governance principles, norms and practices applicable to NPS organizations are not necessarily relevant to all entities with the legally defined not-for-profit (LDNFP) status.

For example, some organizations with the LDNFP status do not have a public-service mandate. Others are not strongly impacted by 'publicness' phenomena. Some do not have two bottom lines. And still others operate as unincorporated associations.

These *non*NPS-organizational characteristics are not inconsequential. In the case of the *non*NPS enterprises involved, such features may render inapplicable or less valid some of the book's prescriptions and proscriptions.

Academics, researchers and consultants have not isolated for special examination the enterprises that comprise the universe of NPS institutions. In most oral and written public discussion, the subcategory of organizations with the LDNFP status with which the book deals is treated as an undistinguished part of a so-called 'independent sector,' or 'nonprofit world,' or 'third America.' Consequently, NPS organizations, as a class, are not well understood—in terms of their uniqueness and crucial importance within our global society.

While this book does not focus specifically on these broader academic and theoretical themes, it is premised on six propositions of a theoretical nature and three inferences drawn from the propositions. **Appendix 2** of the book includes that material. Academics and researchers interested in the theoretical foundation that undergirds the book's chapter presentations may examine **Appendix 2** first.

I fear that events concerning NPS organizations may be outrunning our understanding of their nature, dynamics, and potentials. Therefore, throughout the book I highlight the important issue of the critical need to recognize the distinctive attributes of NPS organizations, which make governing them an endeavor essentially or significantly different from governing other entities with the LDNFP status.

In some manner all chapters of the book emphasize the significance of distinctive facets in the nature of NPS organizations that provide the context and justification for governing them in special if not unique ways.

Because of the nature of their public-interest commitments, because of their multiple and complex relationships with government agencies and programs, because the well being of millions of people depend so significantly on the products and services they provide, and because of the critical roles they play in helping to keep our core institutions viable, vibrant and democratic--NPS organizations have substantial dimensions of *publicness*.

In the book's Introduction I offer a brief explanation of *publicness* phenomena. The point I emphasize here is that NPS organizations face more complex 'publicness' challenges than other organizations with the LDNFP status. Thus many of the broad generalizations in the practitioner and scholarly literature and in public discourse about '*the* nonprofit sector' often gloss over special, and sometimes very difficult, governance challenges and opportunities of boards of directors of NPS organizations.

I was motivated to write the book partly because of my strong belief that the time has come for more thoughtful reflection on how NPS organizations must be governed—not just managed, even as important as management is. It seems to me that there is an urgent need for reappraisal of roles and responsibilities of boards of directors, specifically in the institutional context of NPS organizations, rather than in the generalized setting of nonprofit organizations.

Society needs reasoned decisions concerning the appropriateness of present institutional arrangements involving NPS organizations. It also needs sound judgments regarding issues of whether these arrangements properly reflect essential governing board functions. I hope the book, through its fusion of relevant organization theory and some nontraditional conceptual frameworks, will move us faster toward achieving the decisions and judgments just mentioned.

I have written the book mainly for two types of audience: a primary one and a secondary one.

My primary audience consists largely of the hundreds of thousand of men and women who serve as members of governing boards of NPS organizations. With respect to them my main objective is twofold:

- To foster the development of *learning* cultures within the boardrooms of NPS organizations; and
- To encourage and facilitate thinking about the NPS organization, and the related governance functions, with different mindsets than those set historically by conventional concepts of the nonprofit organization.

A wide range of individuals and groups comprise this book's secondary audience. They include:

- Academics who teach college and university courses in the field of organization cybernetics;

- Undergraduate and graduate students pursuing degrees in general management in college and university nonprofit organization leadership programs;
- Consultants who advise governing board members and executive managers of NPS organizations;
- Media writers and commentators whose beat is the world of organizations; and
- Executives of government agencies and foundations that 'fund' NPS organizations.

In the book, I do not offer these audiences a set of rules for achieving what Phillip Crosby once described a "the eternally successful organization." However, I do present some *prescriptions* for effective and responsible governing behaviors on the part of members of boards of directors of NPS organizations.

My prescriptions are derived in large part from a basic premise: **In the NPS organization, governing behaviors are different, both theoretically and practically, from managing decisions and actions.**

As I discuss it in the book, in the institutional context of the NPS organization, governance has three distinguishing elements. The *first* is ensuring that an organization has a proper orientation toward the future, as it carries out its public-interest commitments.

The *second* involves accountability for the policies and performance of the organization to all of those for whom or on whose behalf the organization exists.

The *third* element of governance is giving overall leadership, direction and guidance to the organization's team of executive managers.

In the NPS organization, as this book conceives it, the governing board is the primary instrument of corporate governance. The board stands midway between the organization's various stakeholders and its team of executive managers. These managers and the members of the board have differing abilities, backgrounds, and personalities.

Specific problems of governance may vary significantly from one NPS organization to another. And over time they may vary greatly within the same NPS organization as a result of dramatic and complex changes in the external environment of the organization. Therefore, it is unlikely that more than a few principles and prescriptions can reasonably be considered generally applicable. The book identifies and discusses the major ones.

Also, what I offer my audiences in this book are some concepts, ideas, and models for board members (and executive managers, too) to examine, reflect on, and internalize. The viewpoints presented are not based on questionnaire surveys, structured interviews, or extensive case studies. Rather, they have grown out of my actual experiences:

- As a federal executive responsible for 'funding,' investing in, and monitoring and evaluating NPS organizations,
- As a board member and officer of many different NPS organizations over a period of thirty-five years,
- As a teacher of organization theory at the Graduate School of Management and Technology at the University of Maryland (University College), and
- As a consultant in organization governance/management to several hundred community-based, regional and national NPS organizations.

It has been my desire to avoid burdening board members and other general readers with a plethora of references. However, I felt a need to assure academic colleagues, researchers, and professional consultants that the main arguments of the book do not ignore relevant principles, premises and models of organization theory. Consequently, I have included quotations and other reference notations whenever I thought they were needed to put my principal themes in a broader context.

I noted at the beginning of this **Preface** that in the early 1960s I was staff director of a special research project for the United Methodist Church's Board of Church and Society. The project involved re-visiting the conventional views on so-called 'separation of church and state' principles, in the light of controversies surrounding the federal government's Headstart, Community Action and other Anti-Poverty Programs. Some of my findings, conclusions and recommendations were presented to the Subcommittee on Constitutional Rights, U. S. Senate Committee on the Judiciary (see Exhibit P-1 below).

I mention this matter here for one reason. Since the chapters of the book were written controversies have erupted over the Bush Administration's Faith-Based Initiatives Program. Several of the central points I highlighted for the Constitutional Rights Subcommittee in March of 1966 are particularly relevant to issues at the core of that administration's Faith-Based Initiatives.

For NPS organizations, apart from any policies of the Bush Administration, the core concerns I highlighted in 1966 have actually become critical governance issues. NPS organizations, by definition, are outside traditional institutions of government. Nevertheless, these organizations have many formalized relationships with government agencies and programs.

This means that NPS organizations are inevitably subject to some degree of government control. The implications of this latter condition pose complex and difficult governance challenges. What kinds of governance systems, processes and personnel are required to prevent government control from undermining the autonomy and distinctive qualities of pioneering and advocacy associated with NPS organizations?

"If vendorism and grantsmanship become the dominant way of life for most [NPS] organizations, who will represent minorities, unpopular or controversial interests, and dissenting views?" (Wolch 1990, xi)

The Bush Administration's faith-based initiatives bring these issues to center stage. Although mentioned in the text, they are not discussed for the reason earlier indicated. However, I hope the discussions presented in Chapters 3 and 4 will point governing board members in some useful directions. In that connection, Exhibit P-1 below should be helpful.

Exhibit P-1

The American people, in seeking to achieve their social goals, seem to be firmly committed to diversity and pluralism, not simply because of the abstract values of private initiative but also because of the demonstrable advantages of actions and decisions at many points throughout the spectrum of American life. Thus we are confronted with a number of complex issues regarding relationships among the multitude of public and private social structures in our society.

The issues we face are strikingly highlighted by such difficult questions as the following: What should be the role of government—Federal, State and local—in relation to private agencies and institutions through which human needs and desires may be satisfied in part? How can patterns of cooperative effort between government and private organizations be developed so as not to undermine the independence, or destroy the initiative, or erode the responsibility and accountability of each? Since private nonprofit agencies and institutions are so prominent a feature of American life, to what extent, under what circumstances, and for what periods of time may government utilize them for achieving public purposes? Are there any circumstances under which private agencies and institutions may be justified in seeking to use public instrumentalities to achieve purposes of the private associations? The difficulty posed by these questions is further compounded by the fact that a great many of the nonprofit private associations scattered so profusely upon the landscape of American institutions either have explicit religious interests themselves, or they are an integral part of other organizations that have such interests. Yet the "religion" clauses of the first amendment commit us constitutionally to the twin values of secular government and religious liberty.

Do the principles of secular civil institutions and religious liberty require governments—Federal, State and local—to make a distinction between private agencies and institutions with explicit religious interests and those that have no such interests? Is the Federal Government precluded from making a loan or grant to a nonprofit agency or institution solely or partly on the grounds that the private organization has explicit religious interests? W. Astor Kirk (March 9, 1966), Prepared Statement Before the Subcommittee on Constitutional Rights, Committee on the Judiciary, United States Senate.

The origins of most NPS organizations that emerged in the 1960s and 1970s are related to certain government policies. Therefore, it is understandable that these new fledgling enterprises developed multiple and complex relationships with government agencies and programs. There were many instances where government agencies and their executive managers became proactive in establishing relationships with NPS organizations.

This development did not escape the attention of the National Center for Voluntary Action. In 1976, ten years after my testimony before the U. S. Senate Subcommittee on Constitutional Rights, that organization engaged Pablo Eisenberg to prepare a paper for the Commission on Private Philanthropy and Public Needs. Eisenberg's paper was originally published in 1977. For the information of the reader, I include Exhibit P-2 below, which contains pertinent comments of Eisenberg relative to the then fledgling NPS organizations.

Exhibit P-2

During the last two decades the number of private organizations engaged n traditional philanthropy, community service, professional betterment, and social activities has multiplied significantly. Paralleling this growth has been the emergence of a new large group of local and national organizations with different purposes and structures and, in some cases, constituencies.

Although all are concerned with major economic and social problems, they may be divided into two major groups. Many organizations combine the characteristics of both types.

The first is primarily involved in the identification, analysis, and resolution of public issues, local, regional, and national. In contrast to the largely middle-class better government and taxpayer groups of the past, the new groups comprise a wide and growing range of concerns and a rich diversity of class and ethnic backgrounds. Civil rights and antipoverty organizations emerged in the 1950s and 1960s, encouraged by increasing citizen responsiveness to social problems and governmental action... Major areas of public needs and services have received attention with the creation of special citizen organizations to deal with housing, wealth, welfare, and community development.

The second type may be characterized as self-determining organizations that have been created to provide disadvantaged constituencies with those opportunities, services, and influences that have not been available through normal or traditional channels. They may involve a particular neighborhood or section of a city, a special minority community or portion of that community, or persons too poor and disconnected to care adequately for their family needs and rights. Their premise is that neither the public nor private sector will pay sufficient attention to their problems and plight, that they themselves must determine and direct their own development. Economic development corporations reflect this avenue for greater economic opportunities for poor and minority communities. So do many of the cooperatives and cottage industries formed in recent years. Other groups and organizations have turned to social and political strategies for greater power and influence. Pablo Eisenberg, *Challenges for Nonprofits and Philanthropy*, 25-26. Edited by Stacy Palmer, © 2005 by the Trustees of Tufts University.

Design of the Book

The book includes an Introduction, seven chapters and three Appendixes. In the Introduction I briefly explain each of the five defining characteristics of the subset of entities with the LDNFP status that the book refers to as NPS organizations. The Introduction also comments on the reason why these organizations must have governing boards.

Chapter 1 is devoted to the critically important role of trusteeship, which we view as much broader in scope than simply a concern with money and property. *Trusteeship* is presented as involving the creation and protection of the NPS organization's legitimacy. I argue in Chapter 1 that the trusteeship aspects of board governance of an NPS organization involve articulating a rationale for the organization's being (i.e., why it exists); determining the source of the authority vested in the organization (and hence to whom it is accountable); deciding on the organization's public-interest commitments (i.e., the social impact it will effect); specifying the manner in which the organization will go about fulfilling such commitments; monitoring organizational performance (in terms of both outcomes and processes); and reporting periodically to those to whom the organization is accountable.

In Chapter 2, I discuss a role of governing boards that involves direction and supervision of the chief staff executive (CSE) of the NPS organization. The book presupposes that within the NPS organization there is a domain of governance and a domain of managing. An aspect of board governance is leading, guiding, directing and controlling the staff executive vested with overall management authority.

Chapter 3 of the book concentrates on the highly important responsibility of governing board members to ensure that the NPS organization becomes and remains a learning organization. This role encompasses board behaviors intentionally engaged in to create a climate, in the words of Senge (1990, 3), "where people continually expand their capacity to create the results they truly desire, where new and expansive patterns of thinking are nurtured, where collective aspiration is set free, and where people are continually learning how to learn together."

The book argues that effective and responsible governance of the NPS organization entails the performance from time to time of catalytic board behaviors. In Chapter 4, I discuss the nature of roles of governing board members, both individually and collectively, which may properly be described as catalytic.

These roles necessitate continually offering challenging visions of desired organizational futures, providing transformational leadership, and maintaining a proactive mindset.

Chapter 5 elaborates on the book's premise that ultimately it is the responsibility of governing board members of the NPS organization to ensure that the organization always has the resources required to achieve board approved goals and objectives. In the chapter, I maintain that it is quite irresponsible for governing board members to adopt or approve specific public-interest commitments for the NPS organization and remain passive with respect to mobilizing the resources needed to fulfill those commitments.

The book acknowledges a widely held view that we live in what Drucker (1968) almost four decades ago characterized as a "society of organizations." The NPS organization exists in an environment filled with many kinds of different entities. Chapter 6 of the book is devoted to a discussion of governing board roles with respect to forging and sustaining inter-organizational linkages and networks, and monitoring the political processes in which the NPS organization is inescapably involved.

Chapter 7, the book's final chapter, examines the important subject of organizational performance evaluation. It argues that, ultimately, governing board members are responsible for to ensuring ongoing systematic assessment of the overall performance of the NPS organization, and for appraising the behavior and effectiveness of the organization's board of directors.

Three appendixes are included in the book. **Appendix 2** contains a succinct statement of the theoretical foundations of the book. I added **Appendix 3** to draw attention to some critical issues of board organization and processes that all NPS organizations need to systematically address.

In 1986, I developed a model of Strategic Governance for board members and executive managers of not-for-profit organizations. The model was published in **Nonprofit Organization Governance:** *A Challenge in Turbulent Times*. Although copies in some form may be obtained through AMAZON.COM, that book is presently out of print.

Whiles this book makes several references to my Strategic Governance model, it does not contain a specific description of the theoretical principles of Strategic Governance, as I espoused them twenty years ago. Since my earlier work may be unavailable to most readers of this book, I include as Exhibit P-3 below pertinent excerpts from *Nonprofit Organization Governance*.

Exhibit P-3

The beginning point of Strategic Governance is recognizing where the governing leaders of an NFP organization stand. Symbolically speaking, they stand in the present with an eye on the future. All of their decisions, all of their actions *must* take place today—at a "now" point in time. Even the development of so-called long-range plans involves *now* or current decisions, based on present facts, present forecasts, present assumptions, and present evaluations of future possibilities and probabilities. But the real consequences of these current decisions and actions will occur tomorrow—at some future date. This phenomenon of "decisions/actions *today* and consequences/effects *tomorrow*" is part of the human condition. It is unavoidable. Eggs laid today hatch tomorrow. Seeds planted now germinate later.

The best way for governing board members and executive managers to deal with the phenomenon of "reaping tomorrow what we sow today" is to systematically analyze possible future consequences of current governing behaviors. This kind of analysis is the first great imperative of Strategic Governance. [It] requires an organization's governing leadership to consciously behave today in ways that are calculated to maximize the opportunities and minimize the limitations and threats that the organization will face tomorrow.

Strategic Governance involves a second great imperative. It is the essential requirement that governing leaders intentionally make decisions and take actions *today* to enhance positive and nullify negative consequences of *yesterday's* commitments.

These two great imperatives really define Strategic Governance—Keeping an NFP organization geared to the future. A strategic thinker/actor is concerned with the fundamental issues affecting the long-term success of the organization as an integrated whole. Governing board members and executive managers who think and act strategically train themselves to recognize the *relationship and significance* of specific current developments, and anticipated future ones, to the long-term success of the organization as a whole; [they] make commitments and formulate policies for coping with and capitalizing on those developments.

Strategic Governance involves "ways of thinking" about the direction an organization *is* taking, and more importantly, the direction it *should* take. Any way of thinking that is appropriate for Strategic Governance is dependent upon some system of strategic analysis and choice.

I use the phrase "strategic analysis and choice" advisedly. The concept that it denotes is not synonymous with the popular notion of "long-range planning. I prefer the phrase "strategic analysis and choice for two reasons. First, it focuses thinking and decisionmaking on substance—on the *type* of cognitive activity rather than on its *time* dimension... Second, the strategic-analysis-and-choice concept necessarily implies *commitment to action,* to making some specified events "come to pass."

Thus, strategic analysis and choice is an approach to identifying and responding to specific forces of environmental turbulence—forces that affect the survival, viability, and success of [NPS] enterprises. "W. Astor Kirk, *Nonprofit Organization Governance: A Challenge in Turbulent Times,* © 1986 by W. Astor Kirk,* 29–31; emphasis in the original.

W. Astor Kirk
Suitland, MD
September 2006

Acknowledgements

One of the ministers of the little rural United Methodist Church in East Texas, where I grew up as child and youth, used to tell the parishioners that our accomplishments could be unlimited, if we were willing to let the Lord get credit for them. Along with the Lord, a lot of earthly people, over a period of more than forty years, should get some credit for this book.

The people who have contributed greatly to my interest in the subject of this book, whose discussions, writings and comments have stimulated my intellectual curiosity, and who have provided many types of personal assistance--all of these people are far too numerous for me to remember by name.

There are five individuals, however, that I am constrained to mention. The first is the late professor Emmett S. Redford of the University of Texas. He quietly displayed some extraordinary moral courage and civility in the late 1940s when I began an effort to desegregate the graduate school of that university to pursue doctoral studies there. In 1950, when I gained admission to the University of Texas, professor Redford became my graduate advisor and, subsequently, the chairman of my dissertation committee. It was from his lectures and his seminar on "public-private federalism" that I first became interested in the governance of nongovernmental organizations that exercise enormous power in our society.

The second individual is Sargent Shriver. Forty years ago, when I was appointed a senior executive of the U.S. Office of Economic Opportunity (OEO), the agency had to address a serious political issue at the Houston, Texas Community Action Agency (CAA). The issue centered on ensuring "maximum feasible participation of the poor," as board members of the CAA. Sargent Shriver was the director of the OEO. On one occasion I had to accompany him to Houston for a meeting with the mayor and city council. During the trip Sargent Shriver put the issue in its proper perspective for me, and his wise counsel shaped my approach to influencing the governance of the new NPS organizations. Sargent Shriver told me that through CAAs we were attempting to effect some fundamental institutional changes in local communities. Then he reminded me of a classic political statement of Niccolo Machiavelli, "There is nothing more difficult to take in hand, more perilous to conduct or more uncertain in its success than to take the lead in the introduction of a new order of things."

The third person I must remember by name is Alexander W. Porter, Esq., a close friend for over fifty years. Throughout the book I mention situations and circumstances I experienced with NPS organizations, as the regional executive of a federal agency. In all of them "Alex" Porter provided competent and wise legal counsel as the regional agency's staff attorney.

The fourth person I am obliged to acknowledge is my son William A. Kirk, Esq.. For over a decade he has served as counsel to a variety of national, regional and local NPS organizations. I have gleaned invaluable insights from our innumerable and in-depth discussions of complex and delicate governance issues he has encountered in counseling his clients.

Last, but obviously not least, is my wife Vivian. As has always been the case during our nearly sixty years of marriage, she went beyond the call of duty to help me in so many ways as I worked on this project. A case in point is the time and care she gave to reading the entire text of the first draft of the manuscript, and offering many very helpful comments and suggestions. Without her constant encouragement and unselfish assistance I could not have completed the research, consultation, and writing that produced the book.

I appreciate enormously the professional assistance of Mrs. Patti Belcher, Acquisition Editor of University Press of America, and Ryan Quick, Editorial assistant of the Rowman & Littlefield Publishing Group.

Naturally, despite the contributions of everyone mentioned here, I alone remain responsible for any errors or omissions in this book.

W.A.K.

Introduction

The organizations that we commonly refer to as 'nonprofits' are actually entities that some government has granted a legally defined not-for-profit ("LDNFP") status. This status specifies certain prescriptions, proscriptions, powers and privileges—**the 4 Ps**. In the case of each organization, these 4 Ps are spelled out in applicable federal and state laws defining its LDNFP status.

The universe of entities with the LDNFP status "encompasses a vast range of organizations, from health-care giants and universities, to nationwide member-serving groups like the Girl Scouts, to advocacy groups like Common Cause and National Right to Life, to religious orders, to an array of locally based associations of every description" (Letts, Ryan and Grossman, 1999, 1).

This book is not about the entire category of organizations with the LDNFP status. Rather, it is concerned with a discrete subcategory. The subcategory involved consists of organizations that, in addition to their LDNFP status, also share the following attributes:

- They are incorporated.
- All of them are nongovernmental entities.
- Each has an acknowledged public-serving mission.
- All have formal relationships with government agencies and programs.
- They are not operated on a commercial basis.

Within the universe of organizations granted the LDNFP status, the ones with these characteristics constitute a distinct species. They are really nongovernmental public-serving organizations. For the sake of convenience and brevity, in the book I refer to them as 'NPS organizations.'

Figure I-1.   Five Dimensions of the NPS Organization

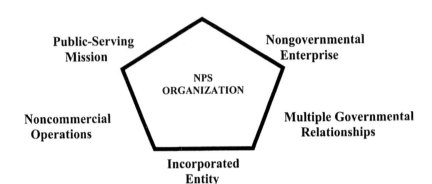

These five defining attributes set the NPS organization apart from the many other types of entities in our society that also have been granted the LDNFP status. Brief explanatory comments on each of these attributes will be presented before turning to the book's primary focus—NPS organization governance.

Incorporation

All entities that we call NPS organizations are incorporated. Indeed, they are corporations, part of 'corporate America.' Most people may not be aware that corporate America includes a lot more organizational forms than those generally recognized as the business corporation. The corporate form of organizing is widely used in all areas of society—in education, religion, the arts, government, the professions, recreation and leisure, labor, fraternal orders, communications, and international intercourse, and so forth, as well as in business and industry.

The classic definition of the corporation, given in 1819 by Chief Justice Marshall, is that it is "an artificial being invisible and intangible and existing only in contemplation of law." The NPS organization is recognized as a separate entity, independent of the persons who govern and manage it. It has a corporate name; it can acquire and dispose of property; it can sue and be sued; and it can execute contracts in its corporate name.

For the NPS organization, the principal advantage of the corporate form is associated with the concept of limited liability. As a separate legal entity, liability is confined to the organization, and does not normally extend to the human persons who govern and manage it. In general, board members will not be held liable for business judgments or financial decisions if these are informed, do not involve a conflict of interest, and do not appear highly irrational.

Nongovernmental

For any organization with the LDNFP status to come under our NPS rubric it must be a nongovernmental enterprise. It must not be part of the formal structure of any government—federal, state, or local. Its employees must not be civil servants. The ultimate control of the affairs of the organization must be vested in its board of director (or possibly in its membership, in those instances where the organization has members who elect the directors).

Public-Serving Mission

All NPS organizations are public-serving entities. They are dedicated to a mission concept that involves serving the general public or broadly defined population groups such as children and youth, persons with physically or mentally challenging conditions, abused spouses, and political refugees. Each NPS organization's fundamental purpose is to tackle a major public problem or a set of interrelated public problems. Each, in other words, exists to serve public interests, to create or produce values for society as a whole.

Therefore, we may say that the 'public-serving' attributes of any entity that qualifies as an NPS organization means that its primary interests are the concerns of persons other than its members, patrons, or sponsors. An organization is a public-serving enterprise if no eligible person is excluded from its benefits as a matter of principle. Conversely, it is not a public-serving entity if otherwise eligible individuals are excluded from its benefits simply because they are not members, patrons, or sponsors of the organization.

Formal Governmental Relationships

All NPS organizations have many "publicness dimensions" (Bozeman, 1987, 5). The publicness dimensions derive not only from dedication to a public-serving mission. They are also associated with the nature and extent of formal relationships that NPS organizations have with agencies and programs of government.

The most crucial of these relationships are those involved in the NPS organization's participation in the implementation of governmental policies, programs and strategies.

During the past four decades, the federal government has initiated a great many social and economic assistance programs. Federal programs like community action, compensatory education, employment and training, model cities, community economic development, and neighborhood renewal not only afforded many opportunities for nongovernmental public-serving organizations to participate in program implementation. They also encouraged such participation through the use of federal financial incentives.

Thus, many patterns of cooperative relationships developed between a host of federal agencies and nonfederal organizations like community action agencies, workforce development boards, community development corporations, and housing assistance corporations. Today, these and other similar enterprises constitute a large universe of NPS organizations that maintain many complex relationships with government—federal, state, and local.

Nearly three decades ago, Charles L. Schultze (1977) described these patterns of cooperative relationships as "the public use of private interest." More recently, Lester M. Salamon (1995) viewed the NPS organizations and the government agencies involved in such relationships as "partners in public service."

Noncommercial Operations

The fifth defining characteristic of the NPS organization is the fact that it is operated on a noncommercial basis. The economic transactions, if any, that it has with its external environment do not produce enough earned revenues to cover the total cost of the organization's operations. Therefore, the organization has to rely on donations, grants, and other forms of subsidy. In other words, the organization funds its work largely through *redistributed* wealth rather than from wealth that the organization creates itself.

Quite a number of NPS organizations do receive some earned revenues—income from fees and other charges for their goods and services. As a response to sharp reductions in government grants and contracts, more are considering this strategy. Throughout the country small groups of NPS organizations are participating in the community-wealth movement, which is a radical departure from deeply ingrained practices that have tied community-based 'nonprofits' to government dollars and private philanthropy. But for most NPS organizations, self-generated revenues are not likely to cover more than a small proportion of their total cost of operation.

Overview of NPS Organizations

The large and diverse group of NPS organizations is multinational, national, regional, statewide (in the United States of America), and local in the scope of their operations. In the United States, a substantial proportion of the locals are community-based enterprises. These American local NPS organizations include such entities as (1) community action agencies, (2) employment and training agencies, (3) community economic development corporations, (4) housing assistance organizations, (5) compensatory education enterprises, (6) health and welfare councils, (7) neighborhood revitalization organizations, (8) small business development corporations, (9) credit counseling services, (10) micro-loan enterprises, (11) charter schools, and (12) neighborhood-based health clinics. These are just a few of the major programmatic types of NPS organizations that operate today in urban and rural communities throughout the United States.

Why did these NPS enterprises emerge and grow on the American institutional landscape? Why are they still in existence? Why are they producing and delivering goods and services that were once produced and delivered almost exclusively by governmental agencies and organizations? There is no single or simple answer to these and similar questions.

In the *Preface* to this book, I noted that the 1960s social activism of the federal government spawned a number of NPS organizations. By 'social activism' I mean the proactive efforts of federal legislative and executive leaders to alleviate not just the symptoms of serious and widespread social problems but also to address their root causes as well. A multitude of legislative and executive program initiatives were launched to combat poverty, educational deficiencies, poor housing conditions, neighborhood deterioration, racial segregation and discrimination, juvenile crime, etc. This effort to overcome massive failures of marketplace capitalism resulted in a national *welfare state*.

In many instances, congressional and executive sponsors of the new governmental initiatives did not believe existing federal, state and local public bureaucracies had the commitment, ability and creativity needed for the successful implementation of the new programs. The alternative was to embrace what Pifer (1967) called "quasi nongovernmental organizations," and what twenty-three years later Wolch (1990) characterized as "a shadow state apparatus."

In this country, over the past twenty-five years, the universe of entities with the LDNFP status has grown enormously. It now numbers over two million organizations. Entities that are exempt from federal income taxation under Section 501(c) (3) of the U. S. Internal Revenue Code are commonly described as *public charities*—a description applicable to some NPS organizations. Today more than 800,000 public charities are registered with the federal Internal Revenue Service. No data are readily available for us to calculate the number of NPS organizations that are public charities, or to make an objective determination of the size of the NPS organization subcategory of the universe of organizations with the LDNFP Status.

However, there is sufficient evidence to warrant a conclusion that the size of this subcategory is not insignificant, that the operations of organizations comprising it affect the well being of tens of millions of Americans, and that the quality of life in hundreds of thousands of local communities throughout the country are impacted by what NPS organizations do or fail to do.

In view of the 'dimensions of publicness' of NPS organizations, some degree of effective governmental oversight of their operations is desirable. Nevertheless, in my view it is essential for these enterprises to create and sustain their own governing systems and processes that can make them more transparent, honest, and accountable to the communities they serve. The critical question is 'Can the quality of board leadership of NPS organizations that the twenty-first century requires be developed and sustained?' That question is a primary focus of this book.

Impact of Publicness

One of the major premises of the book is that collectively the five defining attributes enumerated above produce degrees of publicness far greater in the NPS organization than any associated with other types of 'nonprofits.' Here publicness is conceptualized as the extent to which an NPS organization may exercise political authority or may be directly constrained by political authority. And political authority is viewed as discretion of the organization to make or to refrain from making decisions affecting interests of external individuals and groups. The behavioral consequences of a particular exercise of such discretion are compliance by the affected parties with the asserted imperatives.

The very high level of publicness associated with NPS organizations generates some complex and delicate issues for them. In my view, the most difficult

ones are within the domain of governance rather than in the domain of management. At least three critical governance issue areas stand out.

The first relates to the matter of accountability to major stakeholders for
the policies and performance of the NPS organization.

Second, there is the delicate matter of giving proper overall direction and
policy guidance to the organization's executive management team.

And thirdly, continuous board attention needs to be given the highly important matter of ensuring that the organization stays geared to the future.

Today, all organizations with the LDNFP status have complex external
environments. In the case of the NPS subcategory, the very high level of publicness greatly increases the dimensions and intensity of environmental complexity. Moreover, environmental turbulence is an inescapable fact of life.

A major source of complexity and turbulence is the variety of relationships
that NPS organizations have with multiple government agencies and programs.
Quite often, the differing requirements of these multiple agencies and programs
generate almost irreconcilable conflicts. Such conflicts may negatively impact
vital working arrangements between an NPS organization and constituencies
that it also shares with particular government agencies.

The long-term viability of any NPS organization depends on how clearly
its governing body perceives publicness-generated environmental turbulence,
and how effectively and responsibly that body addresses such turbulence as a
crucial issue of governance rather than a routine management matter.

There is an important distinction between the realm of governance and
the realm of management. Governance usually implies keeping on a straight
course under proper guidance and smooth conduct for the good of the whole
over a long-range period. Governance is concerned with the intrinsic nature,
purpose, integrity, and identity of the [organization], its relevance, continuity,
and fiduciary aspects. In many respects…it is concerned with monitoring and
overseeing of strategic direction, socio-economic and cultural context, resources, externalities, and constituencies of the [organization]. Robert K.
Mueller, *Board Score,* 1982, 15.

You will recall that one of the defining institutional characteristics of each
NPS organization is the fact that it is an incorporated entity. Therefore, the or-

ganization is required by law to have some type of governing body. The book uses the term 'board of directors' (or simply ' board') as a generic reference to this governing body. And the men and women who serve on this body are described as 'board members' or 'directors.'

Simply stated, this book is primarily about the challenging roles and responsibilities the men and women have who serve as members of boards of directors of NPS organizations throughout the United States.

In the book, I argue strongly that the tasks of this group of board members are enormously more difficult than those of their counterparts who serve on boards of entities lacking the institutional features that define the NPS organization. I also contend that this situation is often unrecognized.

All organizations with the LDNFP status must be led, guided, directed and controlled. The book views these functions as governing. Governing is the primary and most important task of directors—acting collectively, as a board.

Not only do NPS organizations constitute a species of enterprises with the LDNFP status. But because they have a substantial degree of publicness, their governance is also a more complex and challenging task than governing other organizations with the LDNFP status. This is due to the critical fact that their publicness has a significant influence on organizational decision-making.

This book grows out of a high priority interest of the author, for more than forty years, in seeking out new ways to improve governance systems and processes of NPS organizations. My interest has been pursued from varying vantage points, including those of graduate school teacher of organization management, senior executive of a federal agency, organization management consultant, interim CEO of three NPS organizations, and board chairperson of several such enterprises.

Three decades ago, Greenleaf (1977) complained about the failure to include board members as "functioning parts" of the leadership of organizations large enough to have full-time paid staffs. About the same time Hage (1980) noted that boards had not been studied often or seriously in traditional organizational literature. He suggested that one reason was that, except in a time of organizational crisis, boards were regarded as inconsequential. There was a widely accepted 'executives-lead' and 'boards-react' paradigm. Two executives crisply stated this principle when they said "Boards react well; they don't create well" (Odendahl and Boris, 1983).

Recently organizational literature has become more aware of boards. However, the conventional taxonomy of organizations does not include NPS organizations. Consequently, while the practitioner related and scholarly literature increasingly discusses board functions, the critical importance of board roles in the NPS organization, as a distinct subcategory of entities with the LDNFP status, remains unexamined.

Over a long period of time I have been engaged in seeking out new ways to improve governance systems and processes within NPS organizations. I have been motivated by a strong conviction of the existence of a critical need to go beyond "emotional rhetoric" (Hage, 1998), beyond "heroic model" images (Herman, 1989, 194–97) and beyond the "beneficence" commitment questions of (Fink, 1989, 112).

I wanted to find a way to convincingly convey a critical message to NPS organization boards. My message is that they (directorates of all NPS enterprises), more than any other types of *nonprofit* boards, operate at the dynamic intersection of (a) strong demands for genuine and enduring public trust and (b) the unrelenting necessity for effective and responsible organizational performance.

As my search unfolded, I was able to identify seven distinct sets of roles and responsibilities that comprise **leading, guiding, directing and controlling** functions (governing behaviors) of board members. These functions are particularly relevant to the unique institutional settings of NPS organizations—within the American political economy today..

My conceptualization of these governing roles and responsibilities accommodates the substantial *publicness* dimensions associated with the NPS organization subcategory of the universe of not-for-profit entities. And it also takes into account the complexities of both the external and internal environments of these organizations.

As Figure I-2 shows, the book devotes a separate chapter to each of the seven sets of governance roles.

Figure I-2. SEVEN SETS OF BOARD ROLES
Chapter, Subject and Board of Directors' Roles/Tasks

---

1. **Trusteeship**
   Board roles/tasks include maintaining legitimacy of organization, establishing relevant purpose, and ensuring effective and ethical organizational behavior.

2. **Managing the Managers**

    Board roles/tasks involve selecting the CSE, providing policy guidance for the CSE, and evaluation of CSE performance.

3. **Facilitating Organizational Learning.**

    Board roles/tasks encompass structured and controlled involvement in the affairs and life of organization outside formal policymaking settings, and serving on ad hoc task forces analyzing key issues.

4. **Performing Catalytic Roles**

    Board roles/tasks involve continually offering challenging visions of a desired organizational future, providing transformational leadership, and maintaining proactive mind-sets.

5. **Equipping the Organization for Work**

    Board roles/tasks require ensuring that the organization has necessary resources to achieve approved goals and objectives.

6. **Establishing and Maintaining Linkages**

    Board roles/tasks include creating and maintaining networks between the organization and other entities in the relevant environment, and monitoring the external political processes in which the organization is involved.

7. **Evaluating Organizational Performance**

    Board roles/tasks consist of systematically assessing overall performance of the organization, and appraising the behavior and effectiveness of the board or directors.

A fundamental premise of the book is that the governing board is an indispensable component of an NPS organization's **leading, guiding, directing and controlling** systems and processes. The expectations of the board, as expressed in both law and organization theory, are captured in the seven sets of roles shown schematically in Figure I-2. Each set is discussed in some depth in one of the following chapters of the book.

To concentrate on 'governing roles' as the organizing concept for the book is a deliberate decision of the author. As I use it in this book, the term *role* refers to organized or structured behaviors—for example, courses of action to be taken or intentionally avoided.

There are a lot of different roles (behaviors) that the board of directors may perform for any given NPS organization. By arranging them in seven affinity groups, I have categorized what I believe are the essential governing behaviors of the NPS board. The nomenclature and language used to identify these affinity groups vary in some important respects from that found in conventional organizational literature. Here, I offer two explanatory comments as possible justification for deviating from the path of conventional practice.

First, I have stated elsewhere in this Introduction my belief that the NPS organization, as the book defines it, does not fit the conventional paradigm of 'nonprofits.' With respect to the NPS organization, many of the key assumptions, premises and models of conventional organizational theory are inadequate, either for explaining its behavior or for improving the quality of its governance.

Second, I share Mueller's (1982, 15) view that there "is an important distinction between the realm of governance and the realm of management." I find unacceptable a large body of conventional wisdom, which appears to hold that governance (*the* task of boards) is merely management writ large. I have chosen some unconventional language, metaphors, rubrics and symbols to focus thought, discussion and debate on governance.

The central themes of the book's discussions center on governance behaviors of NPS organization boards:

- Trusteeship,
- Managing the managers,
- Facilitating organizational learning,
- Performing catalytic roles,
- Equipping the organization for work,
- Establishing and maintaining linkages, and
- Evaluating organizational performance.

While intentionally emphasizing governing board roles, the chapter discussions also recognize and acknowledge the interdependences of the roles of all NPS organization participants. All chapters of the book include some discussion of the reality that decision-making behaviors of board members significantly affect and are in turn greatly affected by the performance of executive management roles. This reality is also captured in the book's explicit advocacy of *strategic governance*—the way NPS organizations deliberately position themselves within their economic and social environments and the methods, tools, and strategies they use to achieve defined outcomes.

Next Chapter

The book elaborates upon my conviction that the NPS organization is a relatively recent and vitally important subcategory of so-called nonprofits. It needs capable and strategic governance as well as good management. Provision of good governance is the task of its board. The chapters that follow lay out in somewhat nontraditional concepts, metaphors, symbols and language what I view as *governing* roles of the NPS organization board.

Thus, I begin with trusteeship in Chapter 1, arguing that strategic governance obliges a board to determine what difference the NPS organization it governs will make in people's lives, how the organization will go about ensuring that intended outcomes occur, and the level of resource utilization that will be acceptable.

Chapter 1

Trusteeship

The enterprises that this book labels as *NPS organizations* comprise a very important subcategory of the expansive universe of organizational entities with a legally defined not-for-profit (LDNFP) status. These organizations exist to produce beneficial social impacts—to make positive differences in the lives of people and to enhance the quality of life of communities. This is the primary reason the general public supports them.

NPS organizations have five defining features: (1) They have public-serving missions; (2) they are not governmentally owned, governed or managed; (3) they have multiple formal relationships with governmental agencies and programs; (4) they are not operated commercially; and (5) they are incorporated entities and exist as not-for-profit *corporations*. In this book, any 'nonprofit' entity that possesses these five characteristics is viewed as an NPS organization.

We begin this chapter by affirming two basic propositions: *First,* whenever the founders of any enterprise choose for it the five defining features of the NPS organization, that enterprise, regardless of its size, thereby incurs inescapably some critical 'trusteeship' obligations.

Second, the governing board, which is the repository of ultimate authority within the organization, necessarily becomes burdened with both a legal and a moral duty to ensure that the enterprise carries out its trusteeship obligations effectively, efficiently and responsibly.

Those two propositions summarize the essential message of this chapter. We will now proceed to elaborate upon that central message.

What Trusteeship Entails

We begin most appropriately with the duty of the governing board of an NPS organization to make sure that the organization properly carries out its *trusteeship* obligations.

But there is a critical question we must answer first: In what sense can we say that an NPS organization has trusteeship obligations? If in fact such obligations exist, what do they include?

The features identified in the book's *Introduction* as 'publicness dimensions' of the NPS organization derive from one fundamental fact. Every NPS organization has received a grant of 'corporate entity' status under the laws of some governmental jurisdiction. *Corporate entity existence* was granted on the basis of assurances from officials of the organization that it would faithfully serve as a *custodian* of specified public interests.

I have long been aware of the fact that the term *public interest* is an elusive one (Kirk, 1958). But when carefully used, this term can convey, in quite meaningful ways, several useful ideas. In the book, I make a conscious attempt to use the term carefully. Thus, I employ the term 'public interest' to refer to some

➤   end condition,
➤   state of affairs, or
➤   pattern of relationships among people, institutions, and things,
       that the members of a polity desire to

◆   REALIZE,
◆   OFFER,
◆   CHANGE, or
◆   PRESERVE.

Here I need to detour for a brief excursion into a dreaded briar patch of political theory. In defining public interest, I used the word 'polity.' I need to explain the sense in which the term polity will be used throughout the book.

I view a *polity* as the most comprehensive social system that serves the needs of members of a particular civil community in accordance with their "share[d] commitment to a set of core values" (Etzioni, 1996, 13).

In the United States of America, such social system may be local, regional or national in scope. It consists of the mosaic of governmental, quasi-governmental and non-governmental institutions by which the members of a given polity organize their common affairs and provide for their own governance. (Cf. Elazar, 1971, 4.)

Now let's get back to the public interest concept. Members of national, state and local polities in this country want an effective antidote for the AIDS virus; they want cocaine usage eliminated; they desire improved performance of public school systems; and they desire to prevent exploitation of children via the Internet. Thus, all of these concerns are current public interests. So also are efforts to move individuals from welfare into productive jobs, to revitalize declining urban neighborhoods, and to eliminate ethnic and racial discrimination. And the list of concerns of members of polities goes on and on ad infinitum.

Every NPS organization must affirm a voluntary commitment to serve as a custodian of some self-defined public interest. And a governmental body endows the organization with communal (including political) authority to protect and/or promote that public interest on behalf of the polity as a whole, or for the benefit of particular, but broadly defined, groups of members.

By cultivating and developing substantial 'publicness' relationships with the governmental institutions of polities, an NPS organization signifies its acceptance of trusteeship obligations, with respect to defined public interests. This means acknowledging and affirming the organization's responsibility to produce social impact—to make a positive difference in the life circumstances of people. It is in this sense that the book views the NPS organization as a trustee.

The trusteeship duty of the board involves clearly articulating public-interest commitments of the NPS organization and ensuring that the organization fulfills those commitments effectively, efficiently and responsibly. The board is ultimately accountable for how well or how poorly the organization performs in this respect. Carver (1990, 35) argues persuasively that this matter is laden with

values about intended impact on the world [and they are] at the root of an organization's reason for existence.

Both the cost and the benefit to the world must be taken into account in considering an organization's transaction with its environment. This most critical of all policy areas concerns itself with what human needs are satisfied, for whom, and at what cost. *The governing board's highest calling is to ensure that the organization produces economically justifiable, properly chosen, well-targeted results.* (Emphasis added.)

I can hardly emphasize too strongly that a crucial aspect of a board's trusteeship duty is to make decisions, after proper deliberation, regarding (a) what positive difference its NPS organization will make in the lives of targeted real people (b) how the organization will go about achieving the intended social impact and (c) at what level of resource utilization.

Of course, the trusteeship aspects of board governance of the NPS organization involves making many other important decisions, including

- Articulating a rationale for the organization's being (i.e., why it exists),
- Determining the source of the authority vested in the organization (and hence to whom it is accountable),
- Deciding on the organization's public-interest commitments (i.e., the social impact the organization will effect),
- Specifying the manner in which the organization will go about fulfilling such commitments,
- Monitoring organizational performance (in terms of both outcomes and processes), and
- Reporting to those to whom the organization is accountable.

Making those types of decisions involves board performance of core tasks of governance.

At any given time, deciding what *end conditions*, what *states of affairs*, and which *patterns of relationships* among people, institutions and things to realize, to preserve, or to change is almost never an easy board task.

That burdensome task usually involves "the performance of [the] political functions of policymaking and resource allocation" (Mueller, 1984, 76), which may require difficult choices among competing stakeholder groups.

It may even entail diplomatically declining to accept grants or other resources, proffered under conditions that would unduly restrict the organization's ability to serve special classes of stakeholders to whom it owes primary allegiance. Buffering the organization from certain pressures of the external environment is what organization theorists call a "boundary-spanning" function. It is included in the governing roles and responsibilities of NPS organization boards. Performing this function can protect an organization from the dangers of vendorism or the surrendering of autonomy to the requirements of government grants and contracts.

Finally, fulfillment of its trusteeship obligations may necessitate that an NPS organization re-design what Eadie (1994, 25) describes as the "leadership mission" of a governing board. (Cf. this book's Chapter 4.)

From time to time, alteration of board culture as well as changes in the mindset of individual board members may be required. This dimension of trusteeship obligations is closely related to performing catalytic roles, which is discussed in much detail in Chapter 3.

Yes, performance of trusteeship roles involves all of these things and more. The critical fact is that boards of NPS organizations are "*the holders of ultimate authority*" (Gross, 1968, 223; emphasis in original work). And "only responsible stewardship can justify a board's considerable authority" (Carver, 1990, 133).

Issues of Legitimacy

In my experience, it is not uncommon for issues bordering on organizational legitimacy to arise in connection with board decision making about what services to provide, for whom, and at what cost. Board governance processes often fail to clearly indicate in whose behalf the board acts or which members of the polity have a first priority claim on public-interest commitments of the NPS organization.

The trusteeship obligations of directors, collectively as boards, involve ensuring and sustaining the legitimacy of their NPS organization.

But what is legitimacy? What does it entail? Local legitimacy consists of a prevailing conviction among members of the local polity that an NPS organization (1) is morally proper, (2) is socially useful, in terms of producing social impact or outcomes that contribute to communal well-being, and (3) is behaviorally beyond reproach, in terms of generally accepted ethical norms of the locality involved (Kirk, 1986, 188–198).

Generally speaking, where such conviction exists, members of a local polity will support the NPS organization—as a matter of reason and principle, and, in some instances, as a collective instrument for promoting social justice.

Quite often boards fail to realize that organizational legitimacy is more than a matter of merely operating within the letter of the law. Meeting legal requirements is, of course, very important. But today it alone is not sufficient to ensure the legitimacy of an NPS organization in any local polity. Boards need a more comprehensive view of organizational legitimacy.

Trusteeship responsibilities of NPS organization boards include generating and sustaining legitimizing convictions about the organizations they serve. This is a vital aspect of a board's ongoing "servant leadership" (Greenleaf, 1977, 91-133), which members of local polities expect.

Within the context of the extensive publicness of NPS organizations, good trusteeship behavior entails an understanding of a critical distinction between power and authority. Board power is simply the capacity to decide and the ability to make decisions prevail, even against opposition.

Board authority is a different matter. It flows from public recognition and acceptance of the moral and ethical principles undergirding institutional roles and behavior. Some of the public outcry a few years ago against certain actions of the federal Internal Revenue Service and several health maintenance organizations, for example, clearly indicate that these institutions can be very powerful and yet have truncated authority.

Legitimacy is the vital link that joins organizational power and organizational authority. It confers authority on the NPS organization, making its decisions regarding policies, priorities, strategies, programs, and allocation of resources 'right' in the eyes of the public.

Once legitimacy is established, and for as long as it exists, it will serve as the most persuasive justification for the exercise of power. On the other hand, challenges to an NPS organization, in terms of questioning its legitimacy, are the most damaging.

During the 1960s and 1970s I became acutely aware of just how damaging such challenges may be. For 14 years I served as the senior executive of Region III of the U. S. Office of Economic Opportunity (OEO). I worked with many community action agencies (CAAs).

At the time CAAs were OEO-sponsored, federally funded NPS organizations. For several years, I was both surprised and puzzled to see so many apparently healthy and well-managed CAAs suddenly face a survival crisis.

After careful examination of many of these situations, I discovered the existence of an *unrecognized latent organizational crisis* (ULOC). I call this phenomenon the 'ULOC Factor. After analyzing and understanding the ULOC Factor, it was then possible for me to identify latent crises in a number of CAAs. Elsewhere [Kirk, 1986, 83] I described ULOC situations in the following language:

> In most of the instances where the ULOC Factor was at work...the governing leaders lacked a clear and articulable concept of the basic social utility

(the end purpose) of the organizations' programs. These leaders were prone to think of their organization in terms of the programs conducted rather than in terms of the [social impact] that should be expected from any programmatic activities.

There was corrosion of the [organizations'] legitimacy. The public was no longer taking their legitimacy for granted. An emerging issue was found to center around the question of whether these organizations had lost the ability to perform up to the level of the public's expectation.

This revisit of my experience with CAAs should alert us to what is likely to happen when boards fail to ensure that organizational programs produce expected social impact. Board directors must guard against simply focusing attention on organizational activities as the principal embodiment of programs. They must ask a fundamental question: **What are the outcomes of the many activities of this organization?** This issue, as my CAA example shows, is also related to the organizational maintenance aspects of trusteeship.

Organizational Integrity

Another equally critical aspect of the trusteeship duty of the board of an NPS organization is to safeguard the integrity of the enterprise. As noted earlier, the corporate *raison d'etre* of an NPS organization is its autonomously defined and stated basic purpose. Over time, the organization's complex governmental relationships, grounded in grants and contracts, may begin to surreptitiously reshape and refocus that self-declared organizational purpose. This is likely to be especially true if the organization's basic purpose is strongly colored with social justice and advocacy values. My experience clearly suggests that the pursuit of different program strategies by two or more governmental agencies can jeopardize the integrity of an NSP organization, as the requirements, expectations and funding resources are manipulated by the different governmental parties to achieve divergent ends.

A cardinal premise of this Chapter is that the board's trusteeship roles include a duty to be proactive with respect to preventing vendorism from impairing or negating the fundamental integrity of the NPS organization.

Organizational Maintenance

So far we have discussed externally focused aspects of the trusteeship roles of boards. These duties also have an internal dimension. It involves leading the NPS organization to achieving and maintaining a well-deserved reputation as a high performance institution whose energies are directed toward effectively fulfilling public-interest commitments consciously chosen by the board.

It should be obvious that here we are talking about high performance not just in financial matters. "Knowing whether and by how much an organization is in the red or black does not speak at all to what the organization is doing well, or whether and how it should be improved" (Letts, Ryan and Grossman, 1999, 35).

A critical aspect of this organizational maintenance task, especially in turbulent environments, is to make sure of an NPS organization's "capacity for survival, to make sure of its structural strength and soundness, of its capacity to survive a blow, to adapt to sudden change, and to avail itself of new opportunities" (Drucker, 1980, 1).

Drucker's comment is about a board's obligations to take leadership in building the adaptive capacity of an organization. This governance task requires the board to constantly keep before it what I call a what's-happening-now picture of the organization, and to examine the implications for the future of insights and signals emanating from this picture.

The trusteeship roles of boards demand that they avoid being driven entirely by what exists. Boards must devote major attention to what they have decided *ought to exist*, with respect to public-interest commitments made on behalf of the NPS organization.

For instance, the core trusteeship duty of legitimizing an NPS organization is not simply to discover a local polity's current vision of public interests, and then determine the best means of promoting it. More than that is involved.

Boards of directors of NPS organizations must endeavor to provide the public with a loftier vision of alternative possibilities, stimulate meaningful deliberations about them, provoke re-examination of current premises and values, and thus broaden the range of potential responses.

As I noted in the *Preface*, NPS organizations constitute a discrete species of the broader category of entities with the LDNFP status. Most enterprises comprising the species emerged as a product of a certain phase of the evolution of the American welfare state, and these not-for-profit entities have a broad mission to seek to bring about change, especially social change that will improve the lives of people.

Board members must realize that making a difference in the lives of people is the real *bottom line* for NPS organizations.

In this regards, trusteeship involves helping the local polity gain a deeper understanding of itself. We will expand on this theme in Chapter 4, as part of the discussion of boards' catalytic roles.

Information Needs of Boards

The prior sections of this chapter have made a case for the proposition that trusteeship roles of the NPS organization's governing board encompass a lot more than traditional concerns about money and property. These roles include decisions and actions with respect to public-interest commitments, organizational legitimacy and organizational viability. Viewing trusteeship roles from this broader perspective raises an issue of the information needs of governing boards.

Board information needs, as well as other requirements, are covered extensively in **Appendix 3**, which deals with designing systems and processes for effective governing board decision-making. I will limit my comments here to some fundamental principles that are not only applicable to trusteeship roles, but also to the other six sets of board roles discussed in Chapters 2 through 7.

In my view, a most basic principle of NPS organization governance is the premise that a governing board is responsible for its own job design. Statutes, articles of incorporation, and administrative regulations provide general rules and establish broad parameters for the governing behavior of boards. But ultimately boards themselves have the responsibility of deciding specifically how they govern their own processes, including how they get needed information.

There exists a popular notion that governing boards may properly delegate the task of creating, evaluating and, when necessary, modifying their job design. My Strategic Governance paradigm (Kirk, 1986, 29–32) is in direct opposition to that viewpoint.

To delegate this function is to allow, for instance, persons and groups without trustee obligations to exercise undue influence in shaping the values that guide governing board trusteeship decision-making. I find that result entirely unacceptable. An NPS governing board, in my view, must explicitly define and clearly articulate its expectations of itself.

When I worked with governing boards of CAAs, as a federal executive grantmaker, I made a diligent effort, with very little success, to persuade them that it was highly inappropriate for them to rely on agency staff executives for board training. I argued that the governing board itself must develop and expressly state the norms of group and individual behavior to which it agrees to hold directors, singly and collectively. And it is the governing board itself, not staff executives, that has the responsibility for properly instructing new board members with respect to these behavioral norms.

Any NPS organization governing board that is serious about the design of its governing systems and processes, including performance of its trusteeship roles, will take the time to do the job itself. The board will, of course, do this job with the participation and collaboration of the chief staff executive (CSE) and his or her top assistants.

We will elaborate these principles in more detail in Chapter 7. Meanwhile, the explanatory comments given here will suffice to guide discussion of the other six sets of governing board roles.

Next Chapter

This book argues that governing the NPS organization is a matter of leading, guiding, directing and controlling it with respect to making and implementing public-interest commitments. The board of directors has ultimate responsibility for these governing processes.

In Chapter 1, I have defined public-interest commitments of NPS organizations as articulated decisions

- regarding consciously chosen social impact,
- intended to benefit targeted members of a polity, which
- are made in the context of a definitive level of resource use.

The chapter discussed trusteeship roles of the governing board, which I viewed as ensuring that public-interest commitments of NPS organizations are carried out effectively, efficiently and responsibly. We now turn to Chapter 2 for an examination of another set of governing board roles—monitoring the performance of the CSE. Adopting the popular title of McSweeney's (1978) book, Chapter 2 refers to this set of board roles as "managing the managers."

Chapter 2

Managing the Managers

In late 1968, I began working on a Strategic Governance model, as part of my efforts to improve the governance of community action agencies (CAAs). At the time they were federally sponsored NPS organizations. As I developed it, the theory of the model includes three fundamental propositions:

First, regardless of size and degree of internal structural differentiation, all NPS organizations have to be led, guided, directed and controlled.

Second, with respect to NPS organizations, this cybernetic process (Gross, 1968, 34) involves two domains: a domain of governance and a domain of executive management.

Third, within the domain of governance, NPS organization governing boards have formal and primary authority; within the domain of executive management, NPS organization chief staff executives (CSEs) have secondary or delegated authority.

For the NPS organizations, the third proposition has some critical implications. For instance, since the board has ultimate formal authority, it is also ultimately responsible and accountable for an NPS organization's *effectiveness* (i.e. its production of beneficial social impacts), *efficiency* (i.e. the ratio of inputs to outputs in its operations), and *responsibleness* (i.e. its adherence to board articulated values).

Moreover, unless constrained by an NPS organization's constitutional document or by applicable statutes and governmental regulations, the governing board is ultimately responsible for defining the breadth and scope of executive-level managing. The board accomplishes such definition through its performance of governing roles.

It is in the contexts just discussed that nonprofit organization literature all too often goes astray. Such literature quite frequently (1) fails to make a distinction between *formal* authority and *informal* authority, and (2) treats 'authority' and 'power' as if they were synonymous concepts. In explaining this book's conceptualization of the board functions of *managing the managers*, a deliberate attempt is made to avoid these mistakes.

Once executive management authority is defined and delegated to the CSE, the governing board has roles that involve monitoring the performance of the CSE in the context of the authority granted to her or him. This chapter discusses those board roles.

In presenting the discussion, the author is always mindful of the fact that this book does not focus on the entire universe of organizations with an LDNFP status, but only with the NPS organization subcategory of that universe. We will commit a critical error if we fail to take into account the five distinguishing attributes of the NPS organization and the special impact that those characteristics may have on board-executive staff relations.

CSE Job Design

Our Strategic Governance model for the NPS organization regards the domain of executive-level managing, although resting on delegated authority, as the CSE's exclusive arena.

It is the CSE who, formally, has charge of the actual day-to-day management of an NPS organization. He or she performs this function under the general direction of the organization's governing board. But since it sits at the apex of the pyramid of formal authority within the NPS organization, the board is accountable for the totality of the organization's affairs.

When NPS governing boards consider establishing a process for monitoring CSE performance, they may choose one or more of several conceivable options. In any case the starting point is deciding the nature and scope of the authority that is to be built into the CSE job design.

Stated conversely, governing boards must first decide how much and which types of their own authority they believe they must exercise directly in order to govern properly and strategically. This is never a one-time decision. Choices made at one point in time will need to be revisited as major changes occur in the external and internal environments of an NPS organization.

In my view, there are two principal ways that NPS organization boards may approach the issue of delegating authority to a CSE. The *first* is to limit CSE authority to that formally and expressly specified in documents duly approved by the board.

The *second* way is to formally affirm or state that the CSE is delegated authority to make any decision and take any action, on behalf of the NPS organization and its public-interest commitments, that the organization's board of directors has not explicitly and exclusively reserved for itself.

Our Strategic Governance model for NPS organizations adopts the latter approach. It is the one that we follow in this book.

This method of governing requires NPS directors to focus on matters and issues, both external and internal, that they believe are of such importance that the board itself should make controlling decisions regarding them.

Here we use the phrase 'controlling decisions' in the sense of dominant, or highest order, or prevailing over all others.

Controlling Decisions and Job Design

Controlling decisions are choices of alternatives, of courses of action, of options, of opportunities, and of strategies that determine directions, shape purpose, serve as reference points, and set limits for other organizational decisions. No non-board action may abrogate or modify them; nor may any non-board choices contradict controlling decisions.

Generally speaking, with respect to NPS organizations, there are two broad categories of controlling decisions. One category includes all decisions primarily aimed at affecting, influencing and/or producing significant or mission-focused events and outcomes in the organization's external environment. Controlling decisions comprising this category are concerned with beneficial social impact. There is a close connection between them and the *raison d'etre* of the NPS organization. Controlling decisions should govern the public-interest commitments of the organization.

The second category of controlling decisions encompasses decisions that are focused internally. They are directed at producing various outcomes (e.g., impacting organizational culture, or creating a new vision, etc.) in the internal environment of the NPS organization.

In everyday language, the term 'policy' is commonly used to refer to controlling decisions, and many other kinds of organizational choices as well. To the extent that controlling decisions are viewed as policy, they must be understood as comprising first-order or primary policy.

For the NPS organization, controlling decisions reveal what the organization believes and what it stands for. Controlling decisions are influenced by those fundamental values of the organization that connect it to a set of basic principles. These principles suggest what *good* NPS organization governance is all about. They include

- A view of the human community and its needs,
- An awareness of deep yearnings of the human soul, and
- Convictions about how people who have and exercise power should behave as members of local polities.

These basic principles also reflect a view of social improvement, of why a particular state of affairs seems better for the local polity than others, and of why the board should prefer an alternative pattern of relationships among people, institutions, and things. And they offer guidance regarding an appropriate structure of authority and power for NPS organizations, given human nature, people's aspirations for communal well-being, and their means of defining and solving public problems.

In the context of the extensive publicness of an NPS organization, issues that should require controlling decisions by its governing board certainly include

1. The organization's public-interest commitments,
2. The members of the polity for whom or on whose behalf these commitments are made,
3. The types and amount of resources that will be used in carrying out such commitments,
4. Approval of partnerships, joint ventures, and other formal inter-organizational agreements, and
5. Organizational practices and performance standards that will be deemed unacceptable.

Decisions about key issues such as these express the principal reasons for an NPS organization's being. They reveal to all stakeholders of the organization the moral, ethical and legal norms that guide how its affairs are and will be conducted. Hence there should be little surprise if controlling decisions regarding these kinds of issues are reserved exclusively for the governing board.

The greater the clarity and precision that a board achieves in stating the types of matters and issues concerning which it will make controlling decisions, the easier it will be for that board to design an authority structure for the CSE job.

◆ **For, at least in theory, the CSE will have what I describe as residual authority.**

Let me illustrate the point by referring to one of my own personal experiences. In 1987, I accepted an appointment as interim CSE of a national agency of the United Methodist Church. The former CSE had resigned abruptly because of serious disagreements among agency senior staff over certain mission and program issues. The authority structure of the CSE was unclear. Unfortunately, the governing board was reluctant to clarify the *policy* situation. Consequently, the former CSE resigned in the midst of a major controversy between several senior managers of the agency.

In order to protect the legitimacy of the agency as well as my own professional integrity, I informed the board in writing, at the end of my first month of service, that henceforth I would proceed on the following premise:

> That, as the agency's chief staff executive, I had formal authority to make any reasonable decision and to take any reasonable actions needed for the overall good of the agency, provided the board has not explicitly said that a given type of decision or action may not be made or taken by the agency's chief staff executive.

Thus I stated in explicit terms my understanding of the formal authority of the CSE of the United Methodist Church agency involved. The board did not quash my particular formulation of such authority. Therefore, the board had both an ethical and a legal basis on which to hold me accountable.

I was responsible for the overall managerial well being of the agency; I had formal authority commensurate with my responsibility; and the board could require me to reveal, explain, and justify any actions that I took or intentionally failed to take.

Our Strategic Governance model for NPS organizations does not treat controlling decisions that explicitly constrain CSE discretion separately from those that do not. Both types are equally important for the purpose of monitoring CSE performance. In either case, the crucial consideration is that both the CSE and the board have the same understanding of the scope of CSE authority.

In an imperfect world, it is inevitable that from time to time there will be situations where the CSE and the board will have different views regarding the scope of CSE authority. Whenever such disagreements do occur, it is the duty of the board to resolve them with prudent dispatch.

Some practitioners and observers will argue that the way to avoid any disagreements between an NPS organization board and a CSE, concerning the scope of authority built into the CSE's job design, is to commit all controlling decisions to written form. Without question, written documents may have tremendous value. But it is highly unlikely that merely reducing controlling decisions to writing can or will prevent any differences of view from occurring.

Written words alone have no meanings. It is people who infuse them with meaning. And individuals may bring varying perspectives and values to the infusion process. Consequently, disagreements may occur at times over interpretations of certain written controlling decisions.

My experience has been that, within the NPS organization, there are two contexts in which varying interpretations of the structure of CSE authority are likely to pose unusual difficulty. The first is where two or more subunits of the board (e.g., officers and committees) strongly express conflicting views, and the CSE is caught in the crossfire.

Two decades ago, the governing board of the National Association for the Advancement of Colored People (NAACP), one of the nation's oldest and most venerable civil rights organizations, was almost destroyed by this type of situation. The crisis was resolved when all factions within the board agreed to support a nationally prominent Congressman for the presidency of the organization. But the candidate refused to take the position until he was given substantial freedom to radically redesign the structure of authority of the CSE job.

There is a second context in which boards of NPS organizations are likely to experience difficulty with respect to authority of the CSE job. It is a situation where differing perspectives are fed by pressures emanating from governmental relationships, especially grantor-grantee relationships. A major feature of the American public policy that has nurtured NPS organizations is a conscious effort by lawmakers and government agencies to specifically impact the governance structures of these organizations.

Some government administrators have program objectives that go beyond achieving diversity in the composition of NPS organization governing boards. They seek to encourage certain board members to perform interest-group advocacy roles. All too often these governmental pressures intensify the usual difficulty of attaining and sustaining consensus concerning issues and matters that should properly be addressed through controlling decisions of the board. Consequently, it is often unlikely that all board members can be persuaded to "agree up front that any position resulting from a fair process is, *and of right, should be,* the position of the board" (Carver, 1990, 189; emphasis in original work).

The central message of the present section of this chapter is that **effective and responsible monitoring of CSE performance, within an NPS organization, begins by designing an appropriate authority structure for the CSE job.** To design such structure requires a comprehensive, coherent and consistent articulation of matters and issues regarding which the board reserves exclusive authority to make controlling decisions.

I argue that whenever and wherever board leadership accomplishes this goal, then the ultimate result will be a *residual authority structure* for the CSE.

This means that the CSE will always know that discretionary authority exists to make any decision or take any action, whether externally or internally focused, and not inconsistent with controlling decisions of the board, that he or she deems necessary to carry out public-interest commitments of the NPS organization.

Board Expectations of the CSE

For the purpose of monitoring CSE performance, the matter of board expectations of the CSE is second in importance only to the CSE job design. A CSE needs (a) to know what is expected of him or her and (b) to have the requisite authority to meet those expectations.

As we begin this section of Chapter 2, a brief statement of certain aspects of the section's theoretical foundation is needed. Over two decades ago, I developed a Strategic Governance model for governing boards and executive managers of NPS organizations. The model defines 'results' as

SOMETHING—
- ➤ **Changed,**
- ➤ **Removed,**

> ➤ **Offered, or**
> ➤ **Preserved** (Kirk, 1986, 51).

In describing the model, I explained that it

> recognizes two types of results: "End" and "Instrumental." Outcomes are an
> NPS organization's End Results; outputs are its Instrumental Results. The out-
> puts must be of such a nature as to cause the outcomes "to come to pass." It is
> the outcomes (End Results) that fulfill the purposes that justify the existence of
> an NPS organization (Kirk, 1986, 50).

A board must state the **End Results (ERs)** that it intends for an NPS organization to accomplish, before it can reasonably express the board's expectations of the organization's CSE. And for responsible monitoring to occur, articulation of such expectations must precede any monitoring activities.

ER Decisions

Monitoring CSE performance, as an aspect of Strategic Governance, requires
stating up front the ERs that NPS organizations will accomplish. I call this function making "ER Decisions." For the NPS organization, ER Decisions define the
"SOMETHING" that the board has decided must be "changed, removed, offered or preserved." The **SOMETHING** is about:

- The positive difference that the NPS organization will make in life
  circumstances of people;
- Concepts of social justice and how the NPS organization will seek
  to get those ideals practically interwoven into the tapestry of major
  public policies and programs;
- The vision and mission that drive the organization;
- The basic values that must govern relations between board and
  staff, among the different staff members, and between all organization participants and the general public;
- How the organization will be accountable to the polities that support it and on whose behalf it operates.

ER Decisions are matters that should be reserved exclusively for governing
boards. ER Decisions enable boards to responsibly formulate expectations of the
CSE, and to develop criteria for monitoring the CSE's performance.

At board development consultations and seminars, participants often tell me that the boards of their NPS organizations will never be able to achieve the level of specificity, with respect to ER decisions, that my Strategic Governance paradigm demands.

My response is simple and quite candid. I tell them that unless their boards attain at least a close approximation of the Strategic Governance model, any talk about responsibly monitoring their CSE's performance is virtually meaningless.

A CSE who agrees to a board monitoring process without insisting on an up-front explanation of what the board's expectations are, is not a very smart CSE. And the members of any given polity are not likely to be well served by an NPS organization whose governing board is unable to articulate expectations of CSE performance, and connect those expectations to accomplishing specific and definable ERs.

It is not uncommon to find boards that believe deciding and expressing a pattern of ERs for their NPS organizations to achieve is a staff function. Whether or not these boards realize it, a troubling implication of this view is that boards work for CSEs.

To allow a CSE and his or her staff to independently make ER Decisions for the organization not only negates board responsibility for determining how CSE monitoring will be carried out. It also amounts to board abdication of critical trusteeship duties, as Chapter 1 of this book defined them.

In the professional literature, there is not a lot of discussion of relationships between boards of directors and CSEs. The little attention that is devoted to the subject often fails to distinguish between *formal authority* and *informal power*. Informal power of CSEs may expand or contract over time, as particular organizational maintenance tasks are variously important at different stages of an NPS organization's life cycle. But the formal authority of the board is a constant, absent changes in state laws and administrative regulations.

The board alone has the authority and the duty to decide definitively what positive social impact an NPS organization must make, for which members of a polity, and at what cost. I do not share the belief held by some governing boards, that they may properly allow the making of ER Decisions to come within the scope of their CSE's residual authority. Ultimately, serious erosion of organizational legitimacy is likely to be an unfortunate consequence of allowing this outcome to occur.

What about boards that avoid genuine governance work by waiting for executive recommendations before they make any ER Decisions? I agree entirely with Carver (1990, 126) who asserts, "When it comes to the long-term, visionary, strategic import of an agency, asking the executive, 'What do you want us to decide?' is not the language of leaders."

Constraints

The Strategic Governance model that this book adopts includes the principle of *residual* authority for the CSE. The principle affirms that the CSE has authority to make any decision and take any action, which is not explicitly proscribed by the governing board, to implement ER decisions of the board.

The principle says to a CSE, in effect, "You may make Instrumental-Results **("IR")** Decisions and take actions in any situation or circumstance as you deem appropriate, so long as what you decide or what you do is not contrary to any board prescription or proscription."

In other words, the board gives approval in advance to any IR Decisions the CSE makes or any activities that he or she gets the organization involved in, provided that boundaries set by the board are not crossed.

In the Strategic Governance model, the making of controlling ER Decisions is reserved exclusively for the governing board. Although the CSE is authorized to make IR Decisions, the board makes controlling ones. Constraints set by the board should typically be in the form of IR Decisions.

It is critically important that a board give very careful consideration (a) to the subject and content components of its IR Decisions that contain CSE constraints, and (b) to the manner of stating such constraints. The primary consideration, in my view, is to ensure that constraints express the board's fundamental values and perspectives regarding executive behaviors, which the board itself believes are imprudent and/or unethical.

In working with CAAs I encountered situations where boards, much too often, acquiesced in constraints on types of executive actions based on funding agency' values and perspectives, rather than their own. What I found most disturbing was the fact that in many of these situations the *agency values* were later discovered to be not those of top executives of the funding agencies but rather the preferences of mid-level program managers.

In crafting constraint-elements of IR Decisions, the beginning point for boards should be at the most general levels. The CSE ought to have as much latitude as practicable for reasonable interpretation of where the boundaries of board constraints are. On the other hand, it is necessary for the board to keep in mind that, at least at the beginning stage, its task is to draft constraint provisions of sufficient breadth to encompass all executive behaviors that the board would find unacceptable.

During the past three decades I have had a fair amount of experience working with NPS organization boards to craft provisions of IR Decisions dealing with 'lobbying,' 'family planning' and 'fee for service' issues. One critical conceptual weakness I have discovered is that most boards manifest a tendency not to distinguish (a) the task of crafting constraint-elements of controlling decisions from (b) the task of devising systems and processes to monitor CSE compliance with constraints. The boards prefer to focus on rules and procedures to make it easy for them to assure 'funding sources' that the NPS organization is in compliance with grant-based constraints.

Monitoring CSE Performance

We can now make the following summative statements about the subject of this chapter—managing the managers:

First, the chief staff executive of the NPS organization is accountable to the governing board (1) for implementing the ER Decisions of the board and (2) for doing so in ways that do not violate the board's constraint decisions.

Second, the board has a duty (a) to establish an authority structure for the CSE job, (b) to make specific ER Decisions and (c) to inform the CSE of the board's expectations concerning accomplishment of these ER Decisions by the organization, and in ways that do not contravene the board's standards of prudent and ethical organizational operations.

Third, once the board has performed this duty, it can then inform the CSE: *Your job performance will be monitored on the basis of the organization's accomplishment of outcomes that implement ER Decisions, and by means that do not violate standards of prudent and ethical organizational conduct set by the board.*

What about monitoring criteria? When a board has made ER Decisions and IR Decisions at a reasonable level of specificity, these decisions comprise practically all the monitoring criteria the board needs. The following examples of an actual ER Decision and a related, specific IR Decision should suffice to illustrate this concept.

♦   **ER Decision**: Maryland Corporation for Enterprise Development (Mcfed) will provide affordable business support services for owners of small enterprises located within the InnerBeltway of the Maryland National Capital Area and serving neighborhoods targeted for revitalization.

♦   **IR Decision:** Mcfed will not provide business support services to enterprises or projects where service fees are insufficient to cover actual costs to Mcfed.

Mcfed is an NPS organization with whom the author is currently working. The board of Mcfed recently made the ER Decision and IR Decision presented above. Those decisions were made during the course of the board's redefinition of the public-interest commitments of Mcfed.

The reader will note that the IR Decision sets constraints on the authority of the organization's CSE. He or she cannot provide business support services where established service fees will be insufficient to cover the actual costs Mcfed will incur. But also note that the CSE still has a very broad discretion with respect to carrying out the specific End Results (social impact) chosen by the board.

Monitoring roles involve setting in advance, for specific ERs chosen, an acceptable performance level, quantitatively and/or qualitatively, for the NPS organization and comparing information reflecting actual achievements with the preset standards to determine that the board's expectations have or have not been met. For example, using the illustration presented above, the board might determine that Mcfed must provide assistance to at least ten firms per year over a five-year period.

The board has to decide which method of monitoring it will use. For example, it might opt for review of internal reports. These documents would be periodic reports from the CSE.

Or, as an alternative, the board may rely on direct inspection. A small committee of the board might be assigned the task of reviewing compliance data and information. A critical caveat should be noted here concerning this method. The committee should not have any authority to direct anyone, and its appraisal must be based solely on stated standards of the board. It must be required to make reports to the full board.

Thirdly, the board might exercise the option of engaging an external audit resource. This approach involves selecting an outside entity to measure CSE accomplishments with respect to specific controlling decisions of the board. It is possible, of course, that the board may wish to employ some combination of two, or even all three, of these monitoring methods.

Governing Board-CSE Relations

Governing board-CSE relationships are very important and delicate matters. They will be discussed in some detail in other chapters of this book. However, a few brief comments on the salient aspects of these relationships—as this book views them—need to be made here in order to accomplish the main purpose of Chapter 2.

The nature, dynamics and societal importance of the NPS organization are such that both its governing board and its CSE are critical components of its cybernetic systems and processes.

With respect to the generation of NPS organizations that grew out of the governmental social activism of the 1960s and 1970s and the new group that emerged in the final two decades of the twentieth century, their formal governance mechanisms include significant and substantive behavioral roles for both board members and CSEs. This means that the quality of working relationships between the board and CSE is crucial. These relationships can seriously affect the effectiveness of the organization's overall performance.

I have served (1) as a consultant to many NPS organizations, (2) as chairman for six years of the board of trustees of a college, (3) as chairman for five years of a 'new generation' NPS organization, (4) as field executive for over sixteen years of a federal agency that funded NPS organizations, and (5) as interim CSE of two community-based NPS organizations.

Those experiences have enabled me to identify some basic principles that can serve as important guidelines for both governing boards and CSEs of NPS organizations. I articulate them here as follows:

First. The focus of the domain of governance, even when critical contributions to its effective functioning are made by the CSE, should remain on those decisions and actions that maintain the NPS organization as a viable human enterprise that achieves a high level of End Results. This is the foundation of its long-term legitimacy. All patterns of relations between the board and the CSE should be viewed and assessed partly in terms of this most important standard.

Second. The governing board is, in the words of Gross (1968, 223), "the holders of ultimate authority." However, some portion of the board's authority has to be regularly exercised on a delegated basis by the CSE. Otherwise, the NPS organization is not likely to perform very well. What authority should be delegated? When should the board intervene in the process of carrying out any delegation? These are perennial issues not easily resolved except as they actually arise in concrete situations.

Third. As an NPS organization moves through its life cycle, it takes on bureaucratic characteristics, just like any other type of enterprise. There are developmental stages in the organization's life cycle where the first duty of the board is "to think with a perspective loftier than is normally possible at the executive levels. . . . [If CSEs] are ahead of the board members in such synoptic views, then the [organization] needs a new board of directors" (Mueller, 1977, 11).

Fourth. There is one characteristic that board members and CSEs should always share. They should have a total (or overall) organizational perspective. In the words of Barnard (1938, 235), they should demonstrate skill in "the sensing of the organization as a whole and the total situation relevant to it." For it is the performance of the entire organization that the board and the CSE are expected to lead, guide, direct, and control.

Fifth. The identify and self-image of an NPS organization need to be reappraised and re-communicated continuously if it is to remain relevant in ever-changing environments. This task is a primary responsibility of both the board and the CSE. Acting separately, neither can perform the task in a satisfactory manner on a sustained basis.

Sixth. How board members and CSEs collectively view the future of an NPS organization is critical. In this connection, "two basically different philosophical stances can be taken: either the future is seen as a projection of the present, which, in turn, is based on the past; or the future is seen as that state of being where one can change the patterns of the present and undo the negatives of the past" (Gawthrop, 1984, 48).

Seventh. Important and sensitive relationships such as those between board members and CSEs depend more on trust, on the inherent necessities of the situation, and on the personality and style of the individuals involved, than on any set of formal rules. One cannot, by drawing vertical and horizontal lines —and little black boxes—on organization charts, capture the most critical dynamics of these relationships.

Eighth. Finally, the major key to the success of a governing board of the NPS organization, even in its relationships with the CSE, is a strong chairperson—an individual who is intelligent, wise, has common sense, and is an excellent leader. Without strong leadership, especially in turbulent times and environments, the board will be inefficient and ineffective. The chairperson should not be biased or prejudiced against either issues or individuals, and should act as an organization leader on the board itself. He or she should understand and use, fairly and wisely, parliamentary procedure and know how to run a meeting officially.

These eight observations are based on my personal experiences in both the boardroom and in the executive suite. They are probably closely akin to Kramer's (1985) "contingency model" of board-executive staff relationships and the theories of Widmer and Houchin (2000). They certainly are consistent with Middleton's (1987, 150) conclusion that "the board-management relationship is a dynamic interaction." It is a challenge for both boards of directors and CSEs and for the other senior managers who are directly accountable to CSEs.

At the beginning of this chapter I stated that my Strategic Governance model for NPS organizations views the domain of management as an exclusive province of CSEs. Since the book focuses on the domain of governance, discussion of executive management functions is beyond its cope. However, it is not inappropriate to state here that I view the general structures and processes of executive-level managing as amenable to IR Decisions of the NPS organization's board of directors. Regardless of the ebb and flow of the informal power of the CSE, the board of directors has formal authority over all of the affairs of an NPS organization. The way in which the board exercises its formal authority is a critical aspect of *governance*.

Next Chapter

In this chapter we have shown that, with respect to leading, guiding, directing and controlling the NPS organization, the domain of executive management must interacts continuously with the domain of governance. The governing board of the organization, through its controlling decisions, determines the structure of authority and responsibility of the CSE who, in turn, is accountable to the board for executive management performance.

Thus, one set of roles of the board, as the chapter explained, is to monitor the performance of the CSE. The difficulty of that task will be considerably lessened if the board carries out effectively its role of facilitating organizational learning. We turn now to Chapter 3 for a discussion of that subject.

Chapter 3

Facilitating Organizational Learning

The problem of developing directors, as presented to me by clients, seems in-
soluble within the bounds set by current organizational thinking. The problem
needs reframing to allow a different and wider perspective. (Robert Garratt,
The Learning Organization, 1987.

An important group of clients for whom I have provided consulting and training
services consists of the core leaders of nongovernmental public-serving (NPS)
organizations. They are the boards of directors and chief staff executives
(CSEs). My experiences in working with this client group for over fifteen years
validate Garratt's insightful conclusions, as expressed in the quotation included
above.

Board directors with whom I have worked in every section of the country
have quite often said to me, both publicly and privately, **"We do not really
know what we are supposed to do--as board members."**

The people who have made this statement, or similar ones, to me come
from all walks of life, from every stratum of American society. As I have ques-
tioned them closely, I found most of them to be sincere in their confessions.
They were really seeking an honest answer to the troubling question "Realistically and practically, what are we supposed to do?"

This book gives seven specific responses to the issue of "What, realistically
and practically, are board members of NPS organizations *supposed* to do?"
Chapter 1 affirmed a collective trusteeship duty of directors to clearly define and

articulate End Results—beneficial social impacts—for NPS organizations to achieve.

Chapter 2 stated that directors of NPS organizations are expected to monitor the performance of chief staff executives (CSEs), with respect to carrying out what are described as *controlling decisions* of the board, within the parameters of board-articulated constraints.

In the present chapter, we will continue our response to the issue just mentioned by examining another set of board roles. This third set involves facilitating the creation and the sustaining of a *learning organization*.

What Is A Learning Organization?

Actually, the term 'learning organization' is a misnomer. The fact is that an organization itself doesn't learn. People, as organization participants, learn. Here I use the concept learning organization purely as a metaphor. Thus, the phrase *learning organization* refers to dynamic and ongoing internal processes of an organization through which its participants continuously enhance their organizationally relevant knowledge, skills and understandings.

In the setting of an NPS organization, these dynamic and ongoing processes create a climate

> where people continually expand their capacity to create the results they truly desire, where new and expansive patterns of thinking are nurtured, where collective aspiration is set free, and where people are continually learning how to learn together (Senge, 1990, 3).

The specific governing task of board directors is to ensure the creation and maintenance of an institutional environment that encourages, nurtures and sustains these processes, consistent with shared values of the NPS organization.

One effective approach to performing this set of roles is for the board to ensure that the board itself has an appropriate culture. An 'appropriate' board culture is one that strongly inspires board members and staff of the NPS organization to make firm *life-long learning (LLL) commitments*. For the sake of convenience and brevity, I shall call these **Triple-L Commitments**.

Within the institutional context of NPS organizations, a Triple L Commitment by an organization participant means that he or she, *inter alia*, always:

- Seeks to understand the systemic consequences of each organizational decision and action,
- Strives to ask the right questions as well as provide the right answers, and
- Attempts to identify and address the underlying causes of problems rather than simply attack their symptoms.

Why A Learning Organization?

During the past two decades, at least, NPS organizations have operated in turbulent environments. There are no good reasons to believe the early decades of this new millennium will bring any relief. On the contrary, the environments of organizations with substantial dimensions of publicness are likely to become more complex and dynamic.

Organizational learning is increasingly being recognized as a critical factor in the ability of all public-serving organizations to produce significant End Results (ERs) in highly turbulent environments (Senge, 1990; Morgan, 1988).

NPS organizations favored with strong Triple-L Commitments by a substantial proportion of board members and staffs tend to be more creative and flexible than those not so favored. Genuine Triple-L Commitments by large numbers of an organization's participants create a learning organization. Kofman & Senge have provided the following insightful descriptions of learning organizations:

> In learning organizations, people are always inquiring into the systemic consequences of their actions, rather than just focusing on local consequences. They can understand the interdependencies underlying complex issues and act with perceptiveness and leverage. They are patient in seeking deeper understanding rather than striking out to "fix" problem symptoms--because they know that most fixes are temporary at best, and often result in more severe problems in the future.
>
> As a result of these capabilities, learning organizations are both more generative and more adaptive than traditional organizations. Because of their commitment, openness, and ability to deal with complexity, people find security not in stability but in the dynamic equilibrium between holding on and letting go--holding on and letting go of beliefs, assumptions, and certainties. What they know takes a second place to what they can learn, and simplistic an-

swers are always less important than penetrating questions (Kofman and Senge, 1993, 33).

Abundant empirical evidence can be marshaled in support of the proposition that NPS enterprises with the attributes of a learning organization, as described by Kofman & Senge, generally outperform by wide margins enterprises without such qualities. Hence one crucial goal of governing boards should be to build into their NPS enterprises the capabilities of a learning organization. This goal can be successfully achieved through governance behaviors, performed on an ongoing basis, that strongly inspire genuine Triple-L Commitments by key organization participants.

Board Culture

In order for any governing board to be effective in performing the role of facilitating and sustaining a learning organization, it must take two critical initial steps. *First*, it must examine its own culture carefully and thoroughly. *Second*, it must eliminate all elements of the board's culture that seriously militate against genuine Triple-L commitments by organization participants.

What are we talking about when we speak of 'board culture?' And how does a board's culture influence Triple-L Commitments of organization participants?

Here I use the term board culture to refer to prevailing values, basic assumptions and beliefs, vivid mental images and dominant interpretations of events that board members hold collectively and deeply. Often operating unconsciously, these largely unexamined presuppositions define in a basic "taken-for-granted" fashion a board's view of itself, and of the NPS organization's environment. They shape board choices, decisions and actions. Thus, a board typically will not seriously consider any ideas, proposals and alternative strategies that run counter to its culture.

Why do I focus here on the culture of an organization's board rather than on the culture of the NPS organization as a whole (i.e., corporate culture)? The answer is straightforward and simple. In my consulting experience, I have found that in most cases corporate culture both reflects and is decisively influenced by board culture.

Thus, the key issue for any NPS organization becomes: Does the board of directors have a culture that anchors on life-long learning? Does it possess a culture that facilitates the organization's adaptation to rapidly changing environments? This, in turn, brings the focus to leadership. I believe it is unlikely that any NPS organization can develop and sustain a genuinely adaptive organizational culture without board leadership.

What should be the driving motivations behind a board's pursuit of a culture that will inspire, encourage and support Triple-L commitments? Is the main purpose simply organizational survival? Is it for reasons associated mainly with public relations? Hardly. I believe there is a more fundamental rationale.

You will recall that in Chapter 1 of this book I outlined a critical governing duty of boards. It is to ensure that NPS organizations make a defined positive difference in the lives of real people, at reasonable costs, and within the bounds of generally accepted ethical and moral standards. If a board has a culture that facilitates building and sustaining an NPS organization as a learning enterprise, then that board is likely to encounter much less difficulty in carrying out the governing duty to which I have just alluded.

Triple-L Commitments are serious business. They involve momentous and far-reaching decisions of organization participants: to continually enhance their knowledge, deepen their understanding, broaden their vision, sharpen their insights, and improve their skills relative to their organization's mission. In an NPS organization, a successful process of inspiring, encouraging and supporting Triple-L Commitments has to begin with the governing board itself.

In my view, evidence of strong Triple-L Commitments should be an essential qualification for all board officer positions within an NPS organization. Officers are special board leaders. They are designers, stewards, and teachers. They are responsible for building boards in which all board members continually expand their capabilities to understand complexity, clarify vision, and improve shared mental models—that is, board officers have a crucial duty to inspire learning.

I argued in Chapters 1 and 2 that the effectiveness of any NPS organization is substantially a function of the overall character and capability of its governing board.

Here I will assert a critical corollary of that premise. Under ordinary circumstances, a governing board will not rise above the level of the leadership competence that generally characterizes the board's officer group. If board officers, as a group, are not passionate about Triple-L Commitments, then the other members of the board are not likely to be either. A board will be unable to effectively facilitate a learning organization in the absence of genuine Triple-L Commitments on the part of most, if not all, board members.

To anticipate and manage external threats in today's environment, contemporary learning organizations must have four skill sets: imagination, cooperative leadership, "learnership," and strategic thinking. Mick Mortlock, "Hurricanes and Learning Organization Obsolescence," *The Public Manager*, Fall 2005, 9.

There are many areas where any NPS organization could be well served by a board that possesses the capabilities of a learning organization. Certainly not the least among those areas is coping with the impact of fundamental, and often sudden, changes in public policies.

By definition, one of the five attributes that distinguish the NPS organization from other organizational entities is its multiplicity of relationships with governmental agencies and programs. These relationships involve grants and contracts, which typically are the source of a substantial proportion of the organization's operating revenues.

Having the capabilities of a learning organization has several important advantages for any board with respect to its dealings with governmental executives and program administrators. Possession of these capabilities, for example, should enable board members to 'sense' in a timely manner emerging issues that are likely to cause shifts in the directions or emphases of government policies and programs. Important governing decisions and actions can be taken in anticipation of probable changes in the governmental marketplace.

Many years ago Martha Derthick (1970) complained about the strong tendency for interactions between NPS organizations and government agencies to become inter-bureaucratic communications. A governing board whose members have genuine Triple-L Commitments is not likely to overlook the need for board directors to have established points of entry into the ongoing communications between their organization and government program executives.

Inter-bureaucratic patterns of communication between NPS organizations and government funders do not sufficiently encompass what Yates (1985, passim) describes as "the politics of management," not to mention the politics of governance. As an executive of a federal government grant-making agency, my experience was that usually communications of an inter-bureaucratic nature tended quite often to gloss over vital issues such as innovation, institutional change, social justice, and the need for what Handy (1990, 225-227) has characterized as "upside-down thinking."

Finally, an NPS enterprise with a governing board that is itself a learning organization has an additional important advantage. Board members are more likely than not to understand the critical implications of the enterprise's dimensions of publicness. Inadequate appreciation of the impact of such dimensions is often a significant factor contributing to board decisions that have serious negative consequences.

Infrastructure for Continuous Learning

The best way of ensuring that organization participants continually enhance their knowledge, skills and understandings is through ongoing encouragement and support of some form of organization infrastructure. Within the domain of governance such infrastructure may be as simple as creating informal fields or spaces where board members, the CSE and the executive managers accountable to the CSE can test new ideas and learn how to inquire together into complex issues, perplexing problems and strategic opportunities.

The 'learning laboratories' about which we speak here need not, and probably should not, be viewed as arrangements associated exclusively with formal policy making activities of the board. Nor should these learning experiences be modeled primarily after classroom-based or highly structured paradigms. Research in adult education increasingly shows that adults, as organization participants, are more likely to learn in sponsored but informal settings. Such research also tends to support the view that more meaningful learning occurs in what some organization theorists describe as *learning communities*. These are essentially informal groups within an organization in which there are no 'experts,' and all group participants are 'inquirers.' Everyone is invited to venture into the realm of curiosity and inquisitiveness together.

As Chapter 5 will discuss, my Strategic Governance model views the board of directors as a *subsystem* of the NPS organization, which, in turn, is viewed as an *open system* within its environment. A board needs to build into its governance processes learning laboratories that allow and assist board members to engage in serious scenario constructions and responses not only 'outside' the system but also 'on' it. Infrastructures for board-member learning require processes that take board members out of the day-to-day pressures into a different kind of space in which they can practice and learn.

> Learning is an autonomous, uncontrollable function of our "human-ness." It just happens. The culture in which this learning occurs—the framework, atmosphere, environment, set of circumstances—is the compelling determinant of the type or quality of the learning. True generative learning is more than the blotting up of information. It is the processing, transformation, and application of that information. The context heavily influences the outcome (Hoffmann and Withers, 1995, 463).

It is the responsibility of the board chairperson, particularly, and board officers in general to play leadership roles in ensuring the presence of very good continuous-learning infrastructures, whatever their nature, within the domain of governance. Staff, of course, may appropriately assist the board. But in my view it is not a primary staff responsibility to promote board development. Carver is absolutely correct when he states,

> The board is responsible for its own development, its own job design, its own discipline, and its own performance. ...[T]his responsibility must be clear to board and staff alike. Primary responsibility for board development does not rest in the chief executive, staff, funding bodies, or government (Carver, 1990, 133).

In the model of Strategic Governance set forth in this book, the rationale for the position just stated is easily comprehensible. Only board members, collectively as a governing body, are the ultimate trustees of the NPS organization. They must make controlling decisions regarding the public-interest commitments of the organization. Consequently, they must bear the primary responsibility for the integrity of its governance.

It is imperative that learning infrastructures, which are focused on governance rather than on management, serve the development needs of board members, especially board members with affirmed Triple L Commitments.

Presently, there is a widespread and urgent need for more learning infrastructures and processes that facilitate fundamental changes in the mental models that board members usually bring to their directorship jobs. Generally speaking board members' mental models are typically based on conventional ideas and beliefs about what is traditionally regarded as the 'nonprofit world.' They are not particularly appropriate for the challenging task of effectively and responsibly governing the species of public-serving institutions that this book describes as NPS organizations.

From my perspective, one critical area where mental models based on conventional concepts of the nonprofit sector fall short is that of resource mobilization. We will address that issue in detail in Chapter 5. Conventional wisdom assigns to the domain of management primary responsibility for attracting unearned resources. That viewpoint is usually reflected in executive-driven infrastructures for board development.

Here we disagree. I believe that ultimately responsibility for attracting unearned resources required for implementing board-approved public-interest commitments lies with the governing board itself.

Because of the extensive dimensions of publicness of the NPS organization, the board cannot appropriately pass on to anyone else the responsibility for ensuring the availability of necessary unearned resources to sustain the programs of the organization—not to the staff, not to a committee, not to an outside consultant or agent.

The board has a duty, also, to establish a policy that the NPS organization as a whole will provide infrastructures to encourage and support Triple-L Commitments by all organization participants. Such policy should be incorporated in controlling decisions (as defined in Chapter 2 of this book) of the board. The organization's CSE has the primary responsibility of ensuring that the policy is effectively implemented. Monitoring the implementation process is a governing duty of the board of directors.

Leadership Factor

The concluding comments that we want to make in this chapter are devoted to reiterating the crucial role of leadership—particularly by the board chairperson and the board officer group.

You will remember we defined a learning organization, at the beginning of Chapter 3, as an enterprise with dynamic and ongoing internal processes that encourage and support organization participants, with respect to the continuous enhancement of their knowledge, skills and understandings.

My experience suggests that very few board chairpersons and other officers adequately appreciate the depth of commitment required to build and sustain NPS organizations as learning enterprises. The type of commitment demanded involves mental models characterized by a significant degree of openness and flexibility.

For board officers and other NPS organization leaders, acquiring really open and flexible mental maps is not always easy to accomplish. In practice, it is disorienting and sometimes deeply humbling, because our mental models of the nonprofit world (or the nonprofit sector) are the basis of the particular 'certainties' that we bring with us to our board positions. We often begin with the illusion that an NPS organization is *indistinguishable* from any other organization with the LDNFP status. Hence the *one-nonprofit-shoe-fits-all-nonprofits* syndrome often shapes our views of the decisions that need to be made and the actions that need to be taken in particular situations.

The taxonomy of organizations used in this book isolates enterprises with five critical organizational characteristics. At least three of the five characteristics—a public-serving mission, *non*commercial operations, a multiplicity of governmental relationships—have highly important implications for board leadership with respect to facilitating Triple L Commitments. Thus, it is evident that commercially run enterprises and governmental agencies and programs exercise significant influence over the flow of financial and other resources to NPS organizations.

The leaders of NPS organizations must recognize the actual and potential nexus between Triple L Commitments and a strategy of innovation as a way of gaining and enhancing continued public support of their enterprises' public-interest commitments. The public-interest commitments of some NPS organizations involve *social-change* goals. It is entirely reasonable for the leaders of these organizations to act on the premise that social change requires organizational learning that alters people's worldview and changes their cognitive models.

Another way to view the leadership factor is to recognize that building and sustaining an NPS organization as a learning enterprise necessitates, as earlier noted in this chapter, a fundamental shift in the cultures (and world views) of their governing boards.

During the past two decades I have had the opportunity of serving as chairperson of the boards of directors of (1) an NPS organization, (2) a not-for-profit community development enterprise, which was not an NPS organization,

(3) a church council and (4) a not-for-profit childcare enterprise. My board chairmanship experiences suggest that to achieve a very modest degree of success in changing conventional mindsets of governing boards requires much patience and forbearance.

It requires, for example, maintaining a precarious and shifting balance between (a) focusing on an organization's End Results decisions and (b) concentrating on making sure that enterprise effectively and responsibly implements those End Results decisions.

Thirty-five years ago Harlan Cleveland wrote a classic little book entitled *The Future Executive.* In that book he perceptively described necessary characteristics of future "Public Executives," by which he meant "people who manage public responsibilities whether in 'public' or 'private' organizations." Cleveland said they would need

> a set of attitudes and aptitudes which seem to be necessary for the leadership of equals...they will be "low-key" people, with soft voices and high boiling points; they will show a talent for consensus and a tolerance for ambiguity; they will have a penchant for unwarranted optimism; and they will find private joy in public responsibility (Cleveland, 1972, 77).

My experiences with the governance of NPS organizations, both as chairperson and as a non-officer board member, suggest that the leadership attributes Cleveland saw as essential for twenty-first century "public executives" are even more critical for governing board officers who are serious about facilitating a learning organization. These officers:

- Must seek board members and other key organization participants who are bright, creative individuals with the curiosity and motivation to try new things.
- Must not hesitate to challenge people to be creative—by questioning traditional approaches and by using meetings as occasions to brainstorm new approaches.
- Must help the organization learn by encouraging people at all levels to engage with others who share similar goals and are addressing similar issues.

In concluding this chapter I can hardly overemphasize my conviction that board officers—as servant leaders—inspire Triple L Commitments and facilitate the building of learning organizations. Collectively, they are the ones 'walking ahead,' encouraging and inspiring other board members and all organization participants to take those steps that are necessary to build an NPS enterprise with the capabilities required to successfully meet future challenges.

Next Chapter

How to achieve and sustain a learning organization is among the most significant issues facing all kinds of public-serving organizations—those with a legally defined not-for-profit status as well as those without such status.

    Throughout this country leaders within both the domain of governance and the domain of management are "wrestling with the questions of how to instill experiences and goals among large groups of people working together in order to insure that things happen in a learning mode" (Kline & Saunders, 1998, 23).

    Here I advocated the proposition that a basic responsibility of the board of directors is facilitating the creating and sustaining of the NPS organization as a learning enterprise.

    In this regard, from time to time the processes that I characterize as Strategic Governance will require the board to act as a catalyst. We turn now to Chapter 4 for a discussion of that subject.

Chapter 4

Performing Catalytic Roles

Any existing organization, whether a business, a church, a labor union, or a hospital, goes down fast if it does not innovate... Not to innovate is the single largest reason for the decline of existing organizations. Peter Drucker, *The New Realities*, 1989, 226–227.

I view a catalyst as a person, group (such as a governing board), or thing that triggers a reaction and participates in it without being consumed in the process.

In this book I affirm the board of directors of the nongovernmental public-serving (NPS) organization as an organized group of people who are collectively endowed with legal authority and entrusted with ultimate responsibility for leading, guiding, directing and controlling the enterprise.

Most of the time the governing activities of the board may be viewed as concerned with keeping the organization on track. That is, in terms of predetermined courses of action. The idea is to keep the organization moving toward achieving what Chapter 2 described as ERs (End Results).

We stated in the previous chapters that accomplishment of specified ERs is the means by which the NPS organization fulfills its public-interest commitments.

Although leading, guiding, directing and controlling behaviors are typically directed at attaining predetermined ERs, occasions do arise that call for a different board focus. For example, in certain situations or under certain circumstances, it may be wise and prudent, if not absolutely necessary, for a board to foster an organizational change of directions.

This chapter deals with the latter type of governing activity. Its purpose is to examine several important dimensions of the board's role as a catalyst. We will attempt to clarify when performing the role of a catalyst is the best and most effective way for the board (a) to carry out its trusteeship obligations, as described in Chapter 1, and (b) to ensure that the organization maintains "a proper perspective on the future" (Handy 1993, 337).

Need for Catalytic Roles

One generalization has gained widespread acceptance in the literature on organizational change. It is the viewpoint that the predominant mode of organizational change is incremental change.

Here I use the concept 'organizational change to mean "either that a new kind of organizational action is undertaken, or that a previous type of action is discontinued, or both" (Brunsson 1985, 10).

Thus, the role of catalyst may properly be associated with any one of Brunsson's three forms of organizational change. For the purposes of this chapter I will view a *catalyst* as a person, group, or thing that (a) causes an organization to undertake a new kind of action, (b) enables an organization to stop acting in some particular way, or (c) is responsible for organization actions involving any combination of "a" and "b."

We know from the research and writings of organization theorists over the past three or four decades that *non-incremental* organizational change processes are not automatic. Quite often such change processes evoke strong resistance from stakeholder groups of all public-serving organizations. As might be expected, there have been several very good studies of the dynamics of "the change resisters" (Odiorne 1981).

As NPS organizations move through their lifecycle stages there will be times when staff executives either fail to recognize a need for a specific type of organizational change or lack the ability to initiate it. These are the times when it is most critical that the board of directors perform the role of a catalyst. It is certainly in these contexts that the board is expected "to think, and think with a perspective loftier than is normally possible at the executive levels of most organizations" (Mueller 1977, 11).

Moreover, these are contexts in which organizational change is a crucial element of organizational effectiveness. The reason is that the change needed "addresses the organization's potential to meet future demands, to take advantage of opportunities and resources within the environment, and to use resources (both human and material) to generate new products and services" (Kanter and Summers 1987, 161–162). More importantly, such contexts may also be those in which failure to initiate and carry out necessary organizational changes will threaten the legitimacy and survival of the organization.

Consider the following example. Community Action Pittsburgh, Incorporated (CAPI) was a large NPS organization with a mission to provide a variety of services in the City of Pittsburgh, Pennsylvania to clients and customers with low incomes. After about ten years of operation CAPI faced an environment in which fundamental organizational changes needed to be made. The necessary changes clearly involved both new kinds of organizational action, and discontinuance of some previous types of action.

In my position as regional director of Region III of the U. S. Community Services Administration, I worked personally with the chief staff executive (CSE) and the board of directors of CAPI for over 18 months. I strongly urged these core leaders to acknowledge the need for several organizational changes, and to creatively initiate and implement them. I made a commitment to increase federal funding to support needed organizational changes.

The board of directors itself was a major part of the problem. Board members had ties to stakeholder groups with which CAPI had formal relationships. Consequently, conflict-of-interest issues arose. The board could not perform the role of catalyst, because it was unable or unwilling to compromise the immediate interests of vocal community groups. Additionally, serious conflicts arose between the board and the CSE. The organization had three CSEs within a one-year period. This meant, among other things, the lack of unity and teamwork within the organization's domain of management.

Without the necessary organizational changes, CAPI progressively deteriorated to a point where all of its funding sources—i.e. all of its subsidy markets—withdrew their support. The organization died.

There are times when it is necessary for the board to perform the role of a catalyst to keep an organization from going down fast. This means board initiation, precipitation, and/or facilitation of organizational changes aimed at ensuring that the organization is structurally strong and sound, that it can withstand a major blow, and ultimately, that it has the capacity for survival.

In addition to keeping any NPS organization in a survival mode, there are two other basic reasons why its board may have to perform catalytic roles from time to time. The first is to make sure that the organization is effective and remains so. Secondly, there is a critical need to keep the organization oriented toward the future.

To you, the reader, what I am about to say may seem a strange contradiction. But the fact is that an NPS organization may have survival capability and yet not be effective. In this sense, effectiveness means accomplishing stated mission and program objectives. It is producing sufficient End Results (ERs) to justify continuing public support.

NPS organization boards face a primary governance challenge that is all too often ignored or overlooked. It is the task of keeping the organization from being caught up in the 'activity trap.' One perceptive observer of this little recognized phenomenon describes it as follows:

> Every [organization] started out to achieve some objective. . . .Resources were assembled. . . .Everyone got busy, engaging in activity designed to carry the organization toward its objectives. But once-clear goals may evolve into something else, while the activity remains the same and becomes an end in itself. The goal moves, but the activity persists and becomes a false goal. This false goal becomes the criterion for making decisions, and the decisions get progressively worse (Ordiorne, 1979, 45).

Performance of catalytic roles by the board may be necessary periodically to help the organization overcome the subtle assumption that an endless stream of activities is always an accurate measure of the accomplishments of organizational ERs.

In considering your organization's appeal for public support, prospective donors are not primarily interested in descriptions of organization activities, no matter how well presented. Rather, their main concern is with the ERs, if any, that these activities have produced or will produce in the future.

Recently, I had a somewhat unsettling experience with the reality behind this principle. At the time I was a member of the board of directors of an NPS organization, which I will call 'Organization X.' Organization X had been in existence for four years. Its stated mission is to create affordable-housing opportunities for low-income residents of the geographical area it serves.

I approached a friend of long standing for a contribution toward the budget goals of Organization X. My friend examined the budget numbers and summary of activities that I gave him. Then he turned to me and asked plaintively: "Astor, where's the beef?"

In asking this metaphorical question, my friend wanted to know what ERs Organization X would accomplish if its budget goals and related activities were realized. In other words, before my friend would make any commitment to support Organization X he required evidence of its intended program output for the fiscal year involved and how this output would be related to the public-interest commitments of the organization.

The situation just described is not an atypical incident. Increasingly prospective donors are focusing on effectiveness, as they feel the pressure of growing competition among organizations for the philanthropic dollar. Thus, periodically it may be necessary for a board to govern catalytically in order to rescue the organization from the activity trap.

Beyond an organization's survival capability and its present effectiveness is another important matter. It is the perennial issue of the organization's readiness for the future. As the noted British expert on organization development, Charles Handy (1993, 337) states, ["maintaining] a proper perspective on the future must be one of the major tasks of the board of any [organization]."

There are times when the performance of catalytic roles by the board is the only practical means of ensuring that an organization maintains a proper perspective on the future. In this context, the most critical aspect of such roles comes into focus. It is when the need exists for the board not merely to initiate organizational change but also to precipitate and facilitate *strategic change.*

For the purposes of this chapter, I view *strategic change* as "nonroutine, nonincremental, and discontinuous change, which alters the overall orientation of the organization and/or components of the organization" (Tichy, 1983, 17).

In this connection, I go against the grain of a well-established tradition in organization theory. That tradition regards the promotion of strategic change as practically an exclusive prerogative of executive managers. This is the position of most theorists and practitioners of "strategic management" (Harvey, 1982; Ansoff, 1979). However, with respect to the NPS organization, I strongly reject the premise that precipitation or stimulation of strategic change is a matter that lies exclusively within the domain of managing. I view it as being included in the overlap between the domains of governing and executive-level managing.

Elsewhere in the present work (Chapter 1) I discussed some critical implications of the substantial dimensions of publicness associated with the NPS organization. Such implications suggest that as any NPS organization moves through the stages of its life cycles, circumstances and situations will occur that impose a duty upon the board to deliberately and intentionally initiate strategic change, even in the face of resistance from executive managers.

In these circumstances and situations, board initiation of strategic change may be the only practical way of keeping the NPS organization geared to the future. Conversely, failure of the board to initiate strategic change may actually contribute greatly to the "going down fast" (Drucker 1989, 227) of an NPS organization.

Consider the following example. Two decades ago I was engaged as a consultant by an NPS entity. I shall refer to the entity here, as 'Organization Y.' Organization Y is a national business and economic research and development enterprise. Its mission is to promote, assist, and expand firms that are owned and/or controlled by African-Americans. At the time I worked with Organization Y, it was entirely locked into the government market. The organization pursued a strategy of concentrating on minority business set-aside programs of the federal government. When the Reagan administration began to systematically phase out or reduce the federal commitment to these programs, this strategy no longer held the same promise for the future.

On several occasions I attempted to persuade the leaders of Organization Y to initiate some strategic changes. I recommended initiatives that involved new service products and new market opportunities. However, neither the executive management team nor the board dared to change the orientation and direction of the organization. Consequently, today Organization Y is far from a viable entity. It is actually in what I have elsewhere described as a "distressed situation" (Kirk 1986, 72).

For a variety of reasons, the governing board of Organization Y has been either unable or unwilling, or both, to perform necessary catalytic roles.

Here my point of emphasis is quite simple. Periodically, strategic change is needed. It may be required to keep an organization geared to the future. In this connection, however, one often encounters difficult attitudinal and philosophical problems in dealing with boards of the NPS organization. Typically, they will tell you that any validity associated with the 'gearing an organization to the future' principle is limited to the business enterprise. Generally, these boards do not believe this principle is relevant in the context of the NPS enterprise. Their focal value is to strengthen the organization's commitment to what it is already doing. Their conventional wisdom seems to tell them that their NPS organization will be tomorrow what it is in the process of becoming today.

However, the realities of today's world have made this conventional idea obsolete. It no longer provides a reasonably safe guide to the future for any NPS organization. In our society today, discontinuous change is a common phenomenon. If what an organization is becoming today is out of line with emergent but critical elements of its environment, it is probably on a collision course with early extinction.

A situation reported in the press sixteen years ago dramatically illustrates the stark reality of this danger. On April 10, 1990, the Washington Post newspaper ran a story under the headline **"KENNEDY CENTER 'BANKRUPT' SAYS NEW CHAIRMAN."** The newly appointed Chairman at the time, James D. Wolfensohn, told a staff writer for the paper that the performing arts center is "bankrupt." He said it had a debt of more than $15 million and faced desperately needed renovation estimated to cost $30 million. Wolfensohn cited poor board performance and inadequate programming as the major culprits.

It appears that the board of directors had adhered to the conventional wisdom that the Kennedy Center enterprise 'will be tomorrow what it is becoming today.' Thus, the Center would continue to be a rental hall in large part, with some concessions to programming. According to board member Roger Stevens, this strategy was very effective "three years ago." The Center was "very solvent and. didn't have any problems." However, it is now obvious that what the enterprise was becoming in 1990 was not geared to the emergent realities of its environment.

Wolfensohn is quoted as having told the staff writer of the Washington Post that the Center "sort of slipped into [its] sad situation" because of a lack of focused programming and strong fundraising support from its board. He added, "If you're deficient in the quality of what you put on, then it is very hard to raise money."

A strong clue to the dynamics of the environment in which the Center exists (the Greater Washington Area) is indicated in the new Chairman's emphasis on the special need to do more to attract the urban population. "The community is not a white Anglo-Saxon community...If you go and look at the Kennedy Center on any given night, it's very hard to find someone other than white persons. It needs to be more accepting and encouraging and welcoming to the community," he said.

The point of emphasis in citing this situation of the Kennedy Center is quite simple, but very important: **Every NPS organization exists within some environment, which is increasingly turbulent, often complex, and some-**

times hostile. **An NPS organization's board of directors, as well as its team of executive managers, must understand this environment from all viewpoints—social, technical, economic, and competitive. Without such understanding, they will be unable to make wise choices and take responsible actions that are consistent with emergent trends.**

In order to ensure the survival and success of any NPS organization in its future environment, board members and executive managers must formulate aggressive strategies of both offense and defense. It is the only way to protect the organization's interests, to make sure it is competitive, and to seize opportunities whenever and wherever they occur. As suggested in Chapter 3, this is a process of managing relationships between the organization and its future environment.

Inevitably, unexpected opportunities and threats will occur, despite careful and systematic planning. An organization cannot afford to ignore the unexpected. It is wiser for any given NPS organization to actively seek out new opportunities than to allow others, with more innovativeness, to grab the best chances that the future will open up.

My affirmation of catalytic roles for the board is based on a basic premise. It is the idea that opportunities have to be seized quickly, even though they may involve risks. There are times when it is necessary for boards to take the initiative and ensure that emerging new opportunities are seized for their NPS organization.

At the beginning of my consulting practice with NPS organizations, I coined the terms *client/customer market* and *donor/subsidy market*. Elsewhere I have discussed them in detail (Kirk, 1986). They are revisited in Chapter 5 of this book. Here I merely want to emphasize the point that these markets constitute critical elements of the NPS organization's environment. The situations of the Kennedy Center, Organization Y, and Organization X, which were described earlier, clearly illustrate this point. It is in connection with the strategies of approaching these markets that the board may need to act catalytically, and initiate, precipitate and facilitate strategic change.

During its heyday the consulting firm of McKinsey and Company coined the term "same-game strategies." That firm's focus was on competitive strategy of the commercially run organization. The term same-game was used to describe strategies that do not change the basic nature and definition of an enterprise in relation to its marketplace. The Kennedy Center, for example, had until recently pursued a same-game strategy. In the 1980s the debilitated state of the NAACP civil rights organization illustrated what can happen when same-game strategies become dysfunctional.

The board of directors of any NPS organization must recognize when continued pursuit of a same-game strategy puts the organization on a collision course with disaster. If the executive management team cannot or will not initiate a strategic change, then the board clearly has a duty to do so.

If the board is, for any reason, unable to discern when an NPS organization faces a critical need for a change of direction, then the board itself is a prime candidate for strategic re-constitution.

The opposites of same-game strategies are new-game ones. The latter are strategies that initiate new undertakings, redefine markets, and seek to build distinctive advantages for the organization. It is critically important for governing boards to recognize when new-game strategies are necessary to sustain an NPS organization's legitimacy as an enterprise whose ERs make a difference in the lives of people and in the quality of life of local polities.

A board performs the role of a catalyst when it discerns an urgent need for the organization to adopt new-game strategies, and then takes appropriate and effective actions to ensure their formulation, adoption and responsible execution.

One of the most difficult problems to deal with is a board that either lacks the ability or is unwilling to respond appropriately to a crucial need for new-game governance. Almost invariably, effective resolution of the problem requires a substantial change in the composition of the board of directors. And this fact is a primary source of the difficulty.

Typically, NPS organizations are non-membership entities. This means that they usually have self-perpetuating boards of directors. If the board directors of a given NPS organization are unable to perform the role of a catalyst, when such performance is necessary, and if they choose not to remedy this deficiency, then there is very little that can be done to really deal with the problem.

Usually a self-appointing directorate has no external authority to which it is directly accountable for poor performance. There is no supervisory membership body that elects directors. Consequently, if a majority of current directors choose to remain in office, thereby maintaining control of the enterprise even though they are ineffective, the feasible options for dealing with this situation are quite limited.

This is precisely the situation at Organization Y, discussed here earlier. Presumably, an appropriate outside person might invoke the intervention of some regulatory body—for example, the state chartering commission or the federal Internal Revenue Service. This might be done if a major regulatory requirement is being ignored. In any event, a practical remedy for this situation is not readily apparent.1

No NPS organization can afford the assumption that its "normal" state of existence is static. Its external environment is dynamic, uncertain, and constantly changing—locally, regionally, nationally, and globally. As was shown in the previous chapter, to cope with this dynamism it is necessary for the board to adopt a proactive stance, rather than rely on reactive behavior.

A proactive stance means that the board must, from time to time, perform the role of a catalyst. At a minimum, the board must be able to clearly explain to all stakeholders of the organization what and where it intends for the enterprise to be five years down the road.

If an organization's governing leaders cannot conceptualize realistic patterns of significant outcomes for it to be producing at least five years from now, either the organization itself is not a viable entity, or it needs a different set of core leaders (Kirk, 1986, 85).

Typically, community-based organizations have cultures containing a deeply rooted negative factor that is most difficult to overcome. It is the persis-

1. At the time of this writing the author is dealing with just such a frustrating situation. The organization with which he is working is ten years old. It is a community development NPS organization that has tremendous *latent* potential. However, it is presently dormant. The board chairman and one other board member are founding directors and they virtually control the organization, which chooses two-thirds of its own directors. They have strongly opposed all efforts to revive the organization, to redefine its mission, to formulate 'new-game' resource mobilization strategies, and to restore the NPS organization's legitimacy. The two 'gate-keeper' board members appear to fear the competition with their own proprietary enterprises that might result from the author's proposed 'new-game' strategies for a revitalization of the NPS organization.

tent attitude that because the organizations have a legally defined not-for-profit status, deciding now *what* and *where* the enterprises should be five years down the road, is not only undesirable; it is also impossible. Each year this attitude is directly responsible for sending thousands of community-based enterprises to organizational graveyards.

During the past thirty years I have had opportunities, as a consultant, to work with many boards of directors and CSEs of community-based NPS organizations. My experiences provide convincing evidence that an effective antidote to the organizational malaise just discussed is the ability and willingness of a board, led by a competent and creative chairperson, to perform catalytic roles. Even where ongoing strategic planning is viewed as an integral component of the CSE's job design (elaborated in Chapter 2), such a board will clearly communicate its expectations to the CSE. The board will ensure that the CSE maintains a proper perspective on the future.

Serving As Catalyst In The Outside World

The reader will recall that one of the five defining attributes of the NPS organization is the fact that it is a public-serving enterprise.

It is established to satisfy expectations, needs or demands of some *polity*, as defined in Chapter 1 of this book.

It has a primary commitment to make a contribution, in some specific way, toward improving the quality of life for people and communities.

Here we describe this mission as the public-interest commitment of the NPS organization.

As any given NPS organization moves through successive stages of its life cycle, there are likely to be times or situations where fulfillment of its public-interest commitments will require the organization to undertake efforts to change societal institutions and processes. But such efforts may not be possible or successful unless the board of directors is able and willing to engage in catalytic behaviors that are focused on the outside world. (Cf. Luke 1998.) This means taking collective actions designed to bring about specific changes in the world beyond the boundaries of the NPS organization itself.

In Chapter 1, I argued strongly that the trusteeship duty of an NPS organization's board goes beyond simply discovering and implementing a local polity's current vision of public interests. I said it also involves providing civic leaders with a loftier vision of other possibilities, and stimulating creative dis-

cussions about them. Thus, carrying out this trusteeship responsibility necessarily entails performing catalytic roles from time to time.

One thing is clearly evident to many thoughtful social observers today. It
is a need for local polities all across America to engage in serious, constructive
public dialogue concerning the nature and requirements of social justice in this
first decade of the twenty-first century. It is essential that the discussion be conducted in a civil manner, and that it cover a wide range of institutional sectors.

For example, the exploration of social justice we have in mind will certainly include education, criminal justice systems, employment and training programs, social welfare, business and economic development, the family structure,
high-technology innovations, civil rights and civil liberties, medical ethics, organized religion, and mass media reporting practices. Such an agenda for NPS
organizations cannot be carried out without catalytic governance by boards of
directors.

You will recall that Chapter 1 conceptualized ERs as
    SOMETHING—
- **Changed,**
- **Removed,**
- **Offered, or**
- **Preserved**

The kind of dialogue referred to above will probably disclose circumstances
where a particular **SOMETHING** may need to be changed, removed, offered or
preserved by appropriate board action in order to achieve a greater measure of
social justice within local polities.

In my view, the NPS organization has emerged as a crucial organizational
expression of the "new realities" (Drucker 1989, 195-206) of our time. In the
United States, this type of institution stands at the threshold of a new American
frontier.

The impact of the NPS organization must be manifest in other creative
ways than innovative delivery of social services. I believe it must be proactive in
opposing unacceptable compromises of social justice in the ongoing processes
of restructuring welfare state policies and programs. In the midst of the inevitable disproportionate distribution of power in American society, the NPS organization must, unceasingly, remind the powerful of the venerable aphorism, "From
those to whom much is given, much is expected." To effectively implement this
aspect of its mission, the NPS organization needs a board of directors able and
willing to behave catalytically when necessary.

For example, the performance of catalytic roles is required to enable the NPS organization to stimulate and facilitate a more open, more public debate about social change, in which consensus can be arrived at 'wholesale' in place of the covert 'retailing' of agreements that now prevails so often in the cloakrooms of legislative halls, in the boardrooms of America's large business corporations, and in the courtrooms of judicial districts. (See Reich 1983, 277.)

A board of directors composed of individuals with diverse backgrounds of knowledge and with a wide range of experience should be able to provide the understandings, insights, and judgment needed for the performance of catalytic roles. But one should recognize that the competencies needed to achieve good day-to-day operational performance are quite different from those required for making sound strategic choices and setting defensible long-term directions.

Organizing for Catalytic Roles

The final part of this chapter's discussion deals with requisite structures and intra-group processes for successful performance of catalytic roles by governing boards of NPS organizations. The presentation here will be abbreviated since much of what is discussed in Chapter 5 is relevant to this concern also.

As indicated in the previous chapter, an anticipatory board culture and individual directors with proactive mindsets are certainly important. However, beyond these attributes there are elements of structure and intra-board processes that impact the performance of catalytic roles.

The board itself is a miniature society. In fact, as the previous chapter stated, it is a subsystem of the whole NPS organization system. Catalytic behaviors are partly a function of interactions and interrelations among all the components of this board subsystem.

No element of structure or process is more critical than the formal and informal arrangements that elicit, facilitate, and sustain creative and robust leadership in the boardroom. Here we view leadership as the art and practice by which chosen individuals influence other members of the board to accept their behavioral preferences, as a means of accomplishing particular ERs.

With respect to the performance of catalytic roles by the board as a whole, there is only one place where this kind of leadership must begin and end. That place is with the officers of the board. In NPS organizations of all sizes, the officer group generally includes a board chairperson, a vice-chairperson, a secretary and a treasurer. This group is the single most important component of the board subsystem.

The quality of strategic leadership provided by the officer group is the primary ingredient or instrument that builds the organization, keeps it geared to the future, and ensures the fulfillment of the organization's public-interest commitments. The strategic capability of the board, as a body, will seldom rise above the level of the strategic vision and competence of the board's officer group. It is critically important that the officer group view the future not merely as an extension of the present, which is based on the past, but as offering opportunities to change the patterns of the present and undo the negatives of the past.

If the officers of any NPS organization lack the requisite vision, commitment, energy, insight, and political skills for catalytic behavior, the board is not likely to perform catalytic roles, except maybe in times of organizational crisis.

Experience has shown that where the officer group is weak and is unable to communicate a strategic vision, it is unlikely that the board will perform catalytic roles that build internal competencies of the organization—its internal technical systems, and their human counterparts. These systems are needed to ensure that the organization acquires and maintains a proper perspective on the future.

From the standpoint of impact potential, as it relates to catalytic behavior, the second most critical component of the board of directors is the executive committee. All large NPS organizations, most middle-sized ones, and many of the small ones have an executive committee. Typically, this committee meets at intervals between regular and special meetings of the board. It is generally empowered to act for the full board in matters that require immediate action or do not involve major issues of policy. It is also the chief coordinating committee of the board, mapping out how the board's business should be conducted, setting agendas, and organizing the activity of other committees. Generally, the organization's officers serve on this committee along with a few other members of the board, some of whom may be chairpersons of other committees.

The presumption is that the executive committee represents the longer-term interests of the organization. Consequently, its members are expected to have a wider perspective than the CSE and other executive managers. Executive committee members are in effect the link between overall governance processes and managerial decision-making, regarding policy interpretation at the highest operating level of the organization. This link is a functional one that is necessary regardless of the size of the organization. Thus, the executive committee represents ongoing board-level interaction with the CSE to assist, as needed, in the implementation of policy and plans.

The point of emphasis here is not a complicated one. It is the fact that the executive committee of the NPS organization is a critical structural element of the board. If this committee does not have a positive orientation towards catalytic action, or if it is unable to behave strategically when necessary and appropriate, then the full board will probably place a very low value on board catalytic roles.

I have had several consulting assignments involving working with boards that actually disvalued catalytic roles because their executive committees viewed such roles as "rocking the boat" behavior. Where the executive committee has a same-game orientation, the board as a whole is unlikely to embark upon any new-game strategies for the organization. The "groupthink" syndrome often prevails (Janis, 1983).

Assume that board officers are able and willing to act as a catalyst when necessary or appropriate. Also assume that the executive committee has the same characteristics. Under these favorable circumstances, what other elements of structure and process are essential for the board of directors to perform as a catalyst?

Within the parameters just assumed, the answer to the question posed is quite simple. The other critical elements are the following: a type of board organization and patterns of interaction among board members, and between the board and the CSE, which facilitate a continuous flow to board members of information that is based on analyzed, evaluated, and summarized data.

This information must be relevant to the two-way responsibility of the board of directors: responsibility focused on (a) the internal needs of the organization and (b) the needs of the broader society reflected in the organization's public-interest commitments.

A central premise of this book is that directors of NPS organizations, collectively as boards, have direct responsibility for the performance of tasks that executive managers, by themselves, cannot be fully relied on to handle well or at all. In discharging this responsibility, boards need to be able and willing to perform catalytic roles when necessary. But boards must have relevant information.

Thus, boards that are properly motivated require the benefits of structures and processes designed to provide the pertinent information needed (a) to cope with the entire range of demand forces, both within and outside NPS organizations, and (b) to build organizations that will fulfill public-interest commitments, receive support from society in return, and therefore survive and grow.

Next Chapter

That NPS organizations operate in turbulent economic, social and political environments is beyond reasonable doubt. Permutations in these environments require appropriate adaptations within the organizations and between them and the larger society of which they are a part.

The governing board is ultimately responsible for the health and well being of NPS organizations. This responsibility includes ensuring that these organizations are adequately resourced, which is the subject of Chapter 5.

Chapter 5

Equipping the Organization for Work

Productive organizations—manufacturing companies, hospitals, commercial banks, and the like—have much in common whether they happen to be corporations in the private sector of society or government agencies in the public sector...[T]hey are of enormous importance to society. They have a strong impact on the social welfare...[T]hey come into being and grow only if they can maintain a balance of exchange favorable to society. In return for giving something to society they receive resource support and political support to survive and grow. Charles Sumner, *Strategic Behavior in Business and Government,* 1980

The job of [leaders] in an organization involves maintaining the evolution of purpose, the recruitment of members, and the balancing of individual inducements with contribution so that the strength of the organization is adequate to its chosen task and the value of its work creates adequate [resources] to maintain the organization. Joseph Bower, *The Two Faces of Management,* 1983.

The two statements just quoted, individually as well as taken together, tell you at the outset what this chapter is all about. And they also summarize at least one-half of the essential argument of this book.

Nongovernmental public-serving (NPS) organizations (a subcategory of Charles Sumner's "productive organizations") have emerged as a vitally important landmark on the American institutional scene. They are of enormous importance to society. The quality of life in society of millions of persons is greatly affected by what NPS organizations do or fail to do.

This fact highlights a critical issue that is indirectly suggested in the above quotation from Joseph Bower. It is an issue that can best be understood by reference to its two essential dimensions.

The first dimension involves the nexus between the societal value of the NPS organization's public-interest commitments and the resources-generating power associated with that value. More closely akin to the language of Bower (1983, 17), this dimension involves the matter of whether "the value of its [the NPS enterprise's] work creates adequate wealth to maintain the organization."

The second dimension of the issue just mentioned revolves around the following question: Where is the locus of responsibility for making sure that the organization achieves "a consistently positive difference" (Ansoff 1973, 54) between the value of resources received from society and the cost of the goods and services used in carrying out the NPS organization's public-interest commitments?

It is my purpose in this chapter to discuss both of these dimensions. In doing so, I will argue that a board's role in equipping an NPS organization involves three basic things:

1. Making sure that the organization's public-interest commitments pertain to or are focused on real needs of society;
2. Making sure that the organization has the resources needed to carry out its public-interest commitments; and
3. Making sure that the organization's resources are used effectively, efficiently and responsibly.

Relevant Public-Interest Commitments

In Chapter 1, I defined *public-interest commitments* in terms of expressly stated decisions (a) regarding consciously chosen positive social impacts, (b) to be made on behalf of specified members of a polity, (c) and accomplished within the context of definitive levels of resource use.

Thus, any NPS organization's public-interest commitments include the societal utilities it has decided to produce and deliver to society. These utilities are both tangible and intangible things that have positive effects on social welfare and on the quality of life in society. They are the means by which NPS organizations accomplish End Results (ERs) and ultimately fulfill their mission.

There is a critical relationship between any NPS organization's public-interest commitments and its legitimacy, as an institution of the local polity in which it operates.

Every organization . . . must function within a context for action that aligns its resources and activities with the underlying economic, social, and technological forces that create its market and define the needs of its stakeholders (Murphy1994, 21).

The first thing that a board of directors must do in equipping an NPS organization for work is to ensure that the organization's public-interest commitments are focused on real and important needs of society. Without a direct and close connection to actual needs of society, the organization's survival in a competitive environment is seriously jeopardized. It is unlikely to secure the resources needed for steady and sound growth.

By definition, NPS organizations are not operated commercially. They do not derive all of their financial and other needed resources from fees for services rendered. They rely substantially on charitable contributions, which, in turn, are based on public trust. The factor of public trust involves transparency and public accountability with respect to the nexus between public-interest commitments and serving important needs of society.

The governing board is the only body within an NPS organization that possesses definitive authority to make this connection exist in the present and to ensure that it will exist in the future.

Because of the attributes of the NPS organization, and because the organization typically operates in turbulent environments, the board increasingly must carry out its responsibilities in an anticipatory and proactive manner.

One of the central theses of this book is that every NPS organization comes into being and exists to satisfy some expectations, demands, or needs of society. If an NPS enterprise survives, it is because the governing leaders of that entity make sure it is successful in actually contributing to the social welfare and quality of life in society. But this theoretical proposition does not give members of the board of directors very much practical indication of what the social welfare is or who society is.

As boards and executive staff of any NPS organization experience the realities of the local polity, they find that there is no such thing as *the* social welfare. Social welfare means different things to different individuals and groups.

Likewise, there is no real entity known   as 'society.' The social fabric of each local polity is made up of many diverse groups, each with its own desires, needs and expectations.

Boards must take into account these differences of value, philosophy, and concerns in deciding which human conditions, and the relative importance of each, that will be addressed through the public-interest commitments of NPS organizations.

This is not a technical problem, calling for a rational solution, at least in the traditional sense. It is a political issue; its resolution requires political leadership.

I use the term *political* here in a non-pejorative sense. I use it in the present context to refer to decisions and actions aimed at influencing the distribution of finite societal utilities where there are common, sometimes overlapping, and often conflicting, claims.

In my experience, such situations are more common than we like to think. With respect to them, staff executives cannot, or should not be expected to, provide the kind of political leadership required to resolve very delicate and high profile issues concerning public-interest commitments for the NPS organization (Kirk 1986, 120-121).

Before any NPS organization begins seriously to consider what its public-interest commitments might be, the board should carefully examine two sets of factors: (a) what the organization's mandates are and (b) who its crucial stakeholders are.

Mandates

The board of directors of any NPS organization will be unable to provide effective leadership, with respect to resolving issues concerning public-interest commitments, unless its members know precisely the mandates under which the organization operates. By mandates I mean 'the musts'—what the organization must do and must not do—that the organization faces.

Before making a decision regarding public-interest commitments and their relation to societal needs, the board should know exactly what external authorities require an NPS organization to do and not to do. Usually these formal mandates are outlined in relevant laws, ordinances, charters, articles of incorporation, contracts, and written agreements. Typically, few board members and executive managers have ever read these documents. It is not surprising therefore that few core leaders are well informed on what the organization is formally mandated to do and not to do.

With respect to deciding public-interest commitments and making choices of ERs, boards and staff executives often make one or both of two fundamental mistakes. "Either they believe they are more tightly constrained in their actions than they are; or they assume that if they are not explicitly told to do something, they are not allowed to do it" (Bryson 1988, 49). For example, board officers and staff executives are especially prone to make these mistakes regarding their organization's legally defined not-for-profit status (LDNFP).

My experiences—as a federal executive, as a management consultant, as a university teacher, and as a board member—suggest that all too often board officers and staff executives think the LDNFP status is more constraining than it actually is. Consequently, they make the fundamental error of assuming, with respect to public-interest commitments, that all organizations with the LDNFP status have identical mandates. Generally speaking, NPS organizations have mandates as 'public charities.' Other not-for-profit organizations do not have mandates that are identical to those of public charities.

That is why, in making decisions about public-interest commitments and their relationships to social welfare and the quality of life in society, clarification of what is not formally ruled out is so important. Alerting board members to what they might decide may lead to valuable discussions about what public-interest commitments ought to be made in particular situations.

All mandates that NPS organizations face are not explicit or formal. Some are informal. Potentially, however, they may be no less important. Informal mandates consist of understandings and verbal agreements that are associated with processes of coalition formation and bargaining, which I will discuss momentarily.

Previous chapters of this book have shown that NPS organizations have a substantial dimension of publicness. Consequently, management of their informal mandates is often a function of political leadership. From my perspective, this fact implies, if not strongly suggests, anticipatory and proactive roles for the board officer group.

Stakeholder Analysis

All NPS organizations have stakeholders. We may define stakeholders as those "groups and individuals who can affect and are affected by the achievement of an organization's mission " (Freeman 1983, 38). Thus, the stakeholders of any NPS organization include public interest groups, protest groups, agencies of government, clients/customers, suppliers, professional or trade associations, and employees.

A stakeholder analysis is an invaluable prelude to decisions about an organization's public-interest commitments or about the ERs to be accomplished. Such analysis is important because the key to success with respect to securing needed resources is satisfaction of major and powerful stakeholder groups.

An NPS organization's board members and CSE should know who such stakeholders are, what standards they use to judge the organization, and how the organization is performing against those standards. In the absence of such knowledge, there is little likelihood that these leaders will know what public-interest commitments will satisfy the organization's stakeholders.

Two examples may prove instructive at this point. The first comes from my experience as chairperson of a board Strategic Planning Committee of a community-based NPS enterprise—a local workforce services corporation. The board directed the Committee to draft a revision of the organization's strategic plan.. During the course of a year the Committee had discussions with several stakeholder groups. Each expressed its views regarding the focus of a revised strategic plan for the organization.

As might be expected, some sharp differences of viewpoint emerged. Near the end of the phase of meeting with groups, the fact became apparent that there would be strong opposition by some influential stakeholders unless a revised strategic plan called for giving special attention to the most severely disadvantaged clients of the organization. Consequently, the strategic plan recommended by the Committee and adopted by the board provided for a public- interest commitment "to give priority attention to clients facing significant barriers to employment."

This public-interest commitment influenced the choices of subsequent ERs by the CSE and board of the organization. Those choices included moving persons from the welfare rolls of the county and into permanent, career-oriented employment. Equally important is the fact that opposition to the strategic plan by influential stakeholder groups was avoided.

The second example is from my experience as treasurer of the Washington Area Community Investment Fund (Fund). As an NPS organization, the Fund is a unique community development enterprise. It is programmatically focused on promoting affordable housing opportunities for low-income residents of the Greater Washington Area. In the 1980s it experienced some difficulty in securing financial resources to cover costs of its management and general support activities, commonly viewed as *administration*.

As treasurer of the Fund, I proposed to the board of directors a concept of a flexible term endowment (FTE) program. The idea was to get individuals and groups to make 'loan investments' in the FTE portfolio, in significant amounts, and at interest rates 50% or less of current market rates. The Fund would then use the loan-investment proceeds to purchase market-rate, secured instruments such as certificates of deposit. The interest differentials would be revenue that the Fund would have to meet part of its management and general support costs.

When I presented this proposal to the board, a number of stakeholder concerns surfaced. The most critical one was a belief that the Fund should 'be clean' in all of its transactions—indirect as well as direct. In this context, being clean meant avoiding receiving money from or investing it with financial institutions believed by some to be 'socially irresponsible.' In order to secure board approval of my proposal, I agreed to a requirement that all aspects of the FTE program must be "consistent with the principles and philosophy" of the Fund.

The point of emphasis in these two examples is that in the process of making decisions about public-interest commitments, the core leaders of an NPS organization must not ignore concerns and demands of key stakeholders.

A concept of Cyert and March (1963) would seem to apply here. In their description of organizational decision-making, they adopted a coalitional view of the processes involved. The coalitional model can illuminate critical interactions that are involved in deciding on public-interest commitments and assessing their relevance for societal needs.

With respect to these decisions, an organization's interactions with stakeholders, and the interactions among stakeholders themselves, do not necessarily proceed from some overarching goal or view of social welfare. Rather, they flow most often "from games among [stakeholder] players who perceive quite different faces of an issue and who differ markedly in the [organization] actions they prefer" (Allison 1971, 175).

Some persons officially connected with an NPS organization must actively build bridges to each key stakeholder group, and they must do so in a systematic way. A major thesis of this book is that the board of directors has a primary responsibility in this matter. The leadership must come from the officer group on the board.

My argument is twofold: *first*, building coalitions with and between powerful stakeholder groups is a political process. It involves equipping the organization for work—not just for today but for the future as well. Achieving success in this process will probably be unlikely in the long term without strong leadership from an authority base outside the executive suite.

The *second* point of my argument is that from the standpoint of strategic governance of the NPS organization, political turbulence must be managed responsibly as well as effectively. Certainly, this entails developing and implementing strategies for interacting with those groups that can affect and are affected by the organization's present public-interest commitments. But equally important, it entails keeping the organization geared to some compelling vision of the future.

Now we are at a point where the major themes of this section of Chapter 5 may be summarized. An NPS organization must have public-interest commitments. Equipping an organization for work includes aligning these commitments with real societal needs. An organization's board of directors has a critical responsibility to make this alignment "come to pass" (Kirk 1986).

Societal needs are not simply a matter of the objective existence of certain human conditions or states of affairs. There is also the crucial matter of perceptions as to whether or not these conditions or states of affairs are social problems. And if they are viewed as social problems, there are likewise perceptions regarding the relative importance of each. All of these perceptions may, and quite often do, vary widely among different stakeholder groups of an organization.

As presented here, conflicting perspectives and opposing demands of different stakeholder groups may appear to be somewhat dry and academic in nature. I attempted to avoid giving that impression by citing a couple of examples. My hope is that these examples will enable you to sense the real impact that stakeholder behavior can have on efforts to align an organization's public-interest commitments with societal needs.

Groups of stakeholders that articulate expectations and make demands regarding these public-interest commitments can be quite serious in their representations. They also have diverse means of enforcing their demands—i.e. rewarding the organization by increasing their support or penalizing the organization by withholding support.

These are the dynamics that create the political context of decision-making with respect to public-interest commitments and generate a critical need for political leadership. That is a major reason why this chapter advocates a proactive role for the board of directors of the NPS organization, when it comes to equipping it for work. That reason will also stand out in the following sections of this chapter.

Mobilizing Resources

Everyone would probably agree that equipping any NPS organization for work includes making sure that it has the resources needed to translate public-interest commitments into ERs. However, general agreement tends to disappear when one goes beyond that simple proposition.

In practice, sharp differences of viewpoint are likely to emerge around two key issues: (1) the location of primary responsibility for seeing that an organization is adequately resourced and (2) the strategies regarded as both most effective and most appropriate for accomplishing any given resource acquisition objectives.

Practical experiences as an organization participant, and the findings of several research studies I have conducted as a consultant, have led me to an important conclusion:

- NPS organizations are not likely to be successful, over the long term, unless there is basic and sustained agreement among their officers with respect to (a) primary responsibility for resource mobilization and (b) appropriate strategies for achieving given resource acquisition objectives.

In the absence of such agreement, any NPS organization will probably be unable to continuously secure adequate resources.

Since this section of Chapter 5 deals with mobilizing resources, perhaps now is the best moment for me to pause and explain briefly my concept of resources.

As I view it here, a *resource* is not limited to money. Rather, it is any aid, device, concept, force, information, symbol, or relationship that an NPS organization uses to produce and/or deliver the goods and services it offers to its clients and customers. It is one of the essential 'input' ingredients of the organization's production process.

In this sense, a resource may be as tangible as a five-dollar bill or a computer, or as intangible as 'goodwill.' So long as a 'thing' of any description is used in the process of producing organization outputs, it is viewed as a resource.

Corporate resources are those assets that form the raw material for the production of an organization's products or services. These include people and managerial talent as well as financial assets, plant facilities, and functional area skills and abilities (Wheelen and Hunger, Second Ed, 1987, 11).

The point I am emphasizing here should not be difficult to understand. Basic and sustained agreement among officers—about resource mobilization responsibilities and about major strategies—is absolutely essential. Otherwise, an NPS organization will not, and probably cannot, obtain adequate resources in the long run. When resource mobilization responsibilities are not identified and intentionally assigned, they tend not to be effectively performed by any organization participant.

Resource Mobilization Responsibilities

For me, resolution of the issue of the locus of responsibility is not difficult, at least in theory. I totally agree with Drucker's (1980, 1) basic premise that the board of directors of an NPS organization has the ultimate responsibility

> to make sure of the institution's capacity for survival, to make sure of its structural strength and soundness, of its capacity to survive a blow, to adapt to sudden change, and to avail itself of new opportunities.

Surely assuring adequate resourcing of the organization is a crucial part of this responsibility. It flows from the fact that the entire board of directors has the legal duty and power to ensure an NPS organization's solvency. Ultimately the board is accountable for the insolvency of an NPS organization.

In my work with NPS organizations, it is surprising how often I encounter situations where guaranteeing the organizations' resource-acquisition effectiveness is not viewed as a primary duty of the board of directors. Rather, board members view this vital task as primarily an important responsibility of the CSE.

For example, the board chairperson of one organization with which I worked recently stated forcefully, "This is an executive director-driven organization. The primary responsibility for raising needed funds is assigned to the executive director." At the time, "Community Developers" (a pseudonym, because the real organization prefers anonymity) faced a financial crisis. It still does. The major reason for its continuing financial plight is the failure of the board to assume any active responsibility for fund-development.

You probably consider money the most essential resource of an NPS organization. You do not stand alone in that view. Generally, board directors all across the country take a similar position. But there is ambiguity concerning whether board roles in equipping the organization for work include a duty to engage in direct, proactive, and supportive behaviors aimed at securing money for the organization.

This book argues that these board roles do, indeed, require such behaviors by board directors. It certainly seems irresponsible for board directors to approve a set of public-interest commitments for the organization they serve and then display an unwillingness to engage directly in behaviors aimed at providing the money needed to carry out such commitments.

Failure of board members to proactively assist in securing necessary funds subtly conveys a strong, if indirect, message to potential donors that the directors do not believe the public-interest commitments and choices of ERs of the organization are important.

If you are a board member of an NPS organization, you have a duty to personally help secure adequate financial resources for the enterprise. This means that you must contribute some cash every year to the organization. How much you contribute is another matter, but there should be no ambiguity about the duty of some sort of annual cash gift. Wolf (1990, 198) noted, "Many funders will be interested in answers to three questions:

1.   What percentage of board members are contributing to an organization (the answer should be 100 percent)?

2.   How much, in total, does the organization receive in board-member contributions (the answer should be a substantial proportion of the total individual contributions--perhaps 20 to 30 percent)?

3.   How active are board members in soliciting funds for the organiza-
     tion (the answer should be very active)?"

Wolf (1990, 198) also reports one contributor as asserting that "'[directors]
are the bellwether. They provide the leadership. If they are not giving gener-
ously themselves, if they are not out there asking for money, the organization is
going to have some problems'."

Board roles of equipping the organization for work impose upon each
board member a duty to proactively assist in resourcing the enterprise, including
making annual cash contributions. How can this obligation be enforced?

I believe the answer to that question must be found in the leadership influence exercised by the officers. As emphasized in Chapters 3 and 4 of this book,
these men and women must set the tone and provide examples for others--for
people in the community, for funders of an NPS organization's programs, for
clients and customers, and for the political leaders of the local polity.

It is the quality of the conceptual, creative, and political behavior of an
NPS organization's core leadership group that determines whether the organization survives, grows, or declines. This group includes officers of the
board of directors, other proactive board members and the CSE and her or his
key subordinate executive managers (Kirk, 1986).

My experience strongly suggests that if an officer group develops and ar-
ticulates a compelling vision of a future for an NPS organization, if they link
public-interest commitments and the board's choices of ERs to that vision, and
if they set examples of cash support, then other board members will generally
behave appropriately. The critical need is for an organization to get proactive
and creative leadership from the officer group of its board. Healthy, vibrant and
high-performance NPS organizations are generally able to recruit and keep this
kind of board officers.

Resource Mobilization Strategies

Assume the existence of a capable and creative board officer group. The
next issue that must be dealt with is the development of an effective but appro-

priate resource mobilization strategy. How will the group go about the business of attracting the resources the organization needs to carry out its public-interest commitments?

Generally speaking, specific elements of resource mobilization strategies are unique to each particular organization and its characteristic environmental setting. However, all strategies derive from and are based on some overall conceptual framework. That framework may be explicit or implicit. Or it may be a combination of both.

This discussion concentrates on a particular perspective. It argues that the conceptual framework presented here is probably more relevant than any others to the unique characteristics and special needs of NPS organizations.

For example, in community-based NPS organizations executive managers and board members generally approach resource mobilization from a *fund-raising* perspective. Essentially their approach to the public is to say, "We believe we are performing good works; therefore you should (or must) support us." Somewhat surprising is the failure of these organization participants to realize the proven weakness of this approach in the highly competitive environments of today. Reliance on a fund-raising approach as the primary strategy is not likely in the long run to produce adequate resources for any NPS organization.

This book proposes a conceptual framework that supports a marketing strategy for resourcing NPS organizations. Let's look briefly at some important dimensions of this framework. **First,** it includes an 'open-system' view of NPS organizations. It sees such organizations as components of a larger society with which they must interact on an ongoing basis. As noted earlier, in interacting with the larger society NPS organizations must be particularly attentive to key stakeholders.

Second, in order for any NPS organization to survive, grow, and be successful, it must give *something* to the larger society and receive something from it in exchange. Broadly speaking, the 'something' given is organization ERs—i.e. positive social impacts—and it receives resources in exchange. In the long run, the economic value of what the organization receives from the larger society must at least equal the economic cost to the organization of what is given. If this equilibrium fails to exist for an appreciable period of time, the organization withers and dies. There is no escape from the harsh reality of this input-output relationship.

Third, in the long run, it is *strategic analysis and choice* that ensures input-output equilibrium. In this connection, strategic refers to specifying in advance the effect the organization intends for current decisions to have on future input-output relationships. The aim is to make those decisions today, whose effects in the future will be to ensure "a consistently positive difference...between costs incurred and the rewards received from the environment" (Ansoff 1973, 54).

There is a **fourth** and final important dimension of the conceptual framework that supports a marketing strategy for resource mobilization. I have already commented on it in Chapters 3 and 4 of this book. All I need to do here is to identify it. For that purpose suffice it to say simply that this fourth dimension involves viewing organizational performance from an 'outside in' rather than an 'inside out' perspective.

For example, board members try to see the organization's outputs, and the public-interest commitments they are supposed to achieve, through the eyes of external stakeholders. A marketing perspective is based on the premise that value is a mental perception in the mind of any NPS organization's resource providers. If they don't understand and experience what organization outputs can do for them, either directly or vicariously, they won't provide resources for such outputs.

Thus, systems concepts, resource dependency principles, strategic analysis and choice, and outside feedback are four strands of a theory of effective resource mobilization. They are woven together, as I now proceed to describe a marketing orientation to guide resource mobilization efforts of NPS organizations. The discussion will show, I hope, that a marketing approach to resource mobilization is significantly more comprehensive in scope than fundraising.

Markets

My advocacy here of a marketing orientation as a guide to effective resource mobilization strategy presupposes a generic concept of markets. But in reality, what is a market? The most general and useful answer is provided by Kotler (1982, 56) when he says that a market is

a distinct group of people and/or organizations that have resources which they want to exchange, or might conceivably be willing to exchange, for distinct benefits.

Any NPS organization must get the resources needed to produce its outputs from some markets, which can be characterized in some way. All markets may be classified in various ways for different purposes. In order to show their connection to resource mobilization, I will divide an NPS organization's markets into two categories: (1) client/customer groups and (2) donor/subsidy groups.

Client/customer groups consist of direct consumers or users of an organization's outputs—hat is, the goods and services it produces of delivers. Donor/subsidy groups include persons and other organizations that do not consume or use these goods and services but who are (or may be) willing, for other reasons, to help cover their production costs.

Since, by definition, an NPS organization is not operated commercially, in practice it must get resources from both of these two types of markets. It is not uncommon for these two market categories to generate conflicting pressures for the board of directors and CSE of an NPS organization. For example, the kinds of products and services clients and customers may demand might not be those that donor/subsidy providers are willing to support.

Exchanges

Any practical concept of an NPS organization as an open system has to include the notion of exchange processes. In order to survive, all open systems must furnish outputs to the environment and receive life-giving feedback and support from the environment. Exchange of its outputs (goods, services, and their accompanying societal utilities) for inputs is the only way the organization can secure necessary support in the long-term.

Another way of stating the exchange relationship between an NPS organization and its markets is to adapt the language used by the renowned organization theorist Herbert Simon (1957, 110–122). All public-serving organizations, whether nongovernmental and commercially run corporations, government agencies, or NPS organizations, must give some inducement to each of those groups (markets) that contribute resources needed by the organization. Thus, according to Simon, NPS organizations must positively influence the "resources-sharing" motivations of their major stakeholders.

[Stakeholder groups] of an organization contribute to the organization in return for inducements that the organization offers them. The contributions of one group are the source of the inducements that the organization offers others. If the sum of the contributions is sufficient, in quantity and kind, to supply the necessary quantity and kinds of inducements, the organization survives and grows; otherwise it shrinks and ultimately disappears unless an equilibrium is reached (Herbert Simon, 1957, 111).

Quid Pro Quo Considerations

At various places in previous chapters I have expressed in different words an important premise of this book: *In order for boards of directors to govern NPS organizations effectively, responsibly and successfully in turbulent environments, the chains of old mindsets must be broken.*

One of my aims here, for instance, is to present the reality of resource mobilization in terms that shatter old mindsets. I want to encourage board members to think in entirely new ways about this task. I want them to understand that quid pro quo considerations are inherent elements of all resource mobilization for their organization.

This is where a marketing-based strategy differs sharply from a fundraising approach. A marketing-based strategy recognizes the necessity for some form of quid pro quo. In other words, nobody gives any NPS organization money without expecting to get **SOMETHING** in return. With respect to donor/subsidy markets, the board and CSE have to figure out what the 'something' (inducement) is that will trigger a desired financial gift.

Inducements will vary between client/customer markets and donor/subsidy ones. And they will also vary among different segments within each market group. Successful resource mobilizers recognize and exploit this critical reality; unsuccessful ones do not. Consider the following vignette, which Thomas Wolf provided in his book on *Managing a Nonprofit Organization:*

> What keeps letters out of the wastebasket? To quote Mrs. Tierney, "I certainly do have favorite charities and their requests are always attended to. But with the others, I take the letter in my hand and as my arm is moving toward the wastebasket, I am scanning the material, checking to see whether there is any personalized message. Has someone handwritten a personal P.S. or is the letter typed to me personally? If not, and now my hand is

very close to the wastebasket, I check to see if I recognize any of the names of people on the board—this list is usually printed on the letterhead, or should be. Finally, I may be struck by the kind of activity the organization is engaged in—the big organizations for cancer or world hunger can't personalize their messages but I support them anyway. In the case of the others, it is the personal aspect of the request that keeps the letter out of the wastebasket. If someone has taken the time to write something, or if one of my friends is on the board, I know I need to be a little more careful. Mind you, this doesn't mean I am going to make a contribution. It just means I will consider it" (Wolf, 1990, 195–196).

The complexity and difficulty of resource mobilization for an organization are increased by the fact that the board and CSE must deal not only with different segments of a given market group. They must also provide appropriate inducements for the two different categories of markets. Inducements that have positive motivational effects within client/customer markets may cause negative effects among donor/subsidy markets, and vice versa (Kirk 1986, 137). For example, in the mid-1960s many client/customers of government-sponsored community action agencies needed and wanted voter registration services. However, federal legislation and regulations prohibited the use of government grant funds for such services.

This market dichotomization is a source of some flexibility for the NPS organization. The policies and procedures compromising its approach to clients and customers may be different from those that the organization markets to donor-investors—providing, of course, that the board and executive managers believe such tactics are both ethical and effective. As noted, however, along with the flexibility, this dual-constituency situation makes the marketing task more complex, since there are two different functions to perform and two different "consumers" to satisfy. But if the organization is to be successful the board must ensure the satisfaction or both parties.

Board Marketing Functions

I emphasized earlier in this chapter my strong belief that at the core of the board roles in equipping any NPS organization for work is the matter of securing the resources needed to fulfill board-approved public-interest commitments. In terms of the conceptual framework discussed here, this means that the board has a marketing function. What is *the* marketing function? Stated simply, it is:

- To create markets for the values (i.e. goods, services, and their general societal benefits) the organization produces, and
- To facilitate exchanges of those values for input resources (i.e. money, facilities, materials, human capital, and "goodwill") the organization needs.

This statement of the marketing function recognizes that an important task of board members is to proactively help develop and retain target markets for an NPS organization's outputs. To have an optimum chance of achieving long-term success, an NPS organization must carefully select target markets. It must avoid quixotic attempts to serve every market and thereby be all things to all people.

Board members and staff executives should consciously distinguish among possible market segments and intelligently decide which ones to offer the organization's outputs. This decision should be based on market potential, choices of ERs, or some other stated criteria. The leaders of far too many NPS organizations have mindsets that lead them to flirt with attempting to do the impossible.

The foregoing statement about the marketing function brings to the forefront another very important issue. What is the first thing board members should do with respect to an organization's offerings? You, the reader, may disagree with me. However, I suggest that board members should first become thoroughly familiar with the "bundles of benefits" and "packages of values" (Kirk 1986, 131) that their organization offers to its chosen markets.

In working with NPS organizations, I find that all too often board members and staff executives have only a hazy idea of their organization's market offerings. They simply are unable to communicate in specific and intelligible language the benefits and values their organizations offer to client/customer and donor/subsidy markets. A massive fuzziness is associated with this whole matter. Consequently, their organizations often fail to get resources that otherwise might be forthcoming.

Much of this fuzziness appears to be an expression of attitudes, assumptions, and beliefs that are associated with old mindsets—that is, paradigms not relevant to twenty-first century realities. For example, many board members and staff executives of NPS organizations argue that outputs in the form of services cannot be defined and described for client/customer and donor/subsidy markets in reasonably specific terms. However, they conveniently overlook or ignore the fact that when services are offered commercially, their principal attributes have to be pinpointed and presented with a relatively high degree of specificity. Individuals and groups are not expected to exchange their financial resources for services offered commercially without specific information about the properties of those services.

Sometime board members and executive managers shift their position. They will argue that an organization with a not-for-profit status (as defined in Chapter 1 of this book) cannot achieve a high level of specificity in presenting its service offering to client/customer and donor/subsidy markets. This argument is patently fallacious.

There is no necessary reason why an organization with a not-for-profit status should be any less capable than one without such status, for example, in specifically describing its family planning services; or its employment and training services; or its childcare services; and so forth. The same technologies for service definition and presentation are as available to organizations with a not-for-profit status as they are to organizations without such status.

The problem is that boards of directors and many staff executives of organizations with the not-for-profit status have 'mental maps' that detour them away from clarity, specificity, and responsibleness in the definition and presentation of their enterprises' service offerings. Too often ambiguity, fuzziness, and at times dissimulation, seem to be accepted as crucial values in governing community-based NPS organizations.

"What has any of this got to do with resource mobilization for any NPS organization?" you may ask. My answer is "Everything."

At some point board members and the CSE of an NPS organization have to determine if any of the resources it needs are going to come from targeted client/customer markets. If so, then they have to decide in what proportion? An organization's performance in these markets will indeed be greatly affected by the way it presents the qualities of the goods and/or services that it offers. As will be discussed momentarily, this issue becomes even more critical in the context of donor/subsidy markets.

Organizations must be more and more mission focused, with a high results orientation. Donors are increasingly seeing themselves as investors, and want to see substantial return on their investment by understanding what their dollars are doing. Annual reports, solicitation materials, and all outreach must be based on the impact of gifts on the long- term needs of the community...

Donors...increasingly feel and express a need to belong: not only through their gifts but [also] by offering their opinions, ideas, counsel. Organizations must be prepared to embrace the donor not only as a source of money, but [also] as a source of guidance. Only then will true partnership be forged, and the magnitude of the investor role be realized (Kay Sprinkle Grace, 1997, 277).

By definition, all NPS organizations are non-commercially conducted. This means that their boards of directors have a responsibility for securing some essential resources elsewhere than from clients/customers. In other words, the organizations must engage in exchanges with donor/subsidy markets.

With respect to the resource mobilization focus of this chapter, all donor/subsidy markets are viewed as having one crucial aspect: They consist of individuals and groups who have no personal knowledge of or experience with the goods and/or services any NPS organizations offer. This lack of direct experience with such output offerings needs to be taken into account in interactions with all donor/subsidy markets.

In popular parlance, we refer to resources obtained from donor/subsidy markets as *contributions, donations,* and *grants*. This reference fails to call attention to the mutual exchange of value that these transactions involve. In other words, the principle of quid pro quo applies to these markets as well as to client/customer ones. If board members have mindsets that eschew this principle, or fail to take it into account in interactions with donor/subsidy markets, then the board is not likely to achieve long-term success in obtaining necessary resources for an NPS organization.

Wolf's vignette, which was presented above, should clearly indicate that individuals and groups do not make donations, gifts, and grants to organizations simply because the organizations needs money. Their benefaction, if any, derives from an expectation of obtaining in return some consideration that has benefits for the donors. These benefits may be social, moral, psychological, or economic in nature. The point of emphasis, however, is not their character but the fact that the benefits are perceived as an existent or potential reality.

At one time or another, most individuals and groups may be viewed as included in an actual or potential donor/subsidy market of some NPS organization.

They have desired or preferred societal ERs—end conditions, states of affairs, or patterns of relationships among people, things and institutions--that they want to "come to pass" (Kirk, 1986, 26).

For these individuals and groups such societal (communal) ERs are the benefits. The output offerings of the organization must, therefore, be 'benefitized' for them. *Benefitizing* is accomplished by demonstrating a connection between a particular client/customer group's consumption or use of the outputs of an NPS organization and the realization of some communal benefits desired or preferred by donors or subsidy providers. In other words, the organization must show that the changes in individuals, groups, or specific societal conditions a potential donor desires will actually occur if the organization's clients and customers consume its products and services

In the Strategic Governance model I developed for NPS organizations, I describe these indirect beneficiaries as *socio-economic investors (SEinvestors^{TM}).* My SEinvestor concept is the equivalent of Grace's (1997) "donor-investor" concept. The theory underlying the motivations of SEinvestors is set forth in **Box 5.1.**

Box 5.1   SEinvestments & SEinvestors

An SEinvestment occurs when a person or an organization, in making a given investment decision, consciously attempts to strike a balance between interest in current *financial returns* and a desire *to make a determinate impact on some particular area of human affairs.*

All investors want to maximize the *utility* associated with each investment decision. Maximum utility is a function of two distinct kinds of return on investments. The first is the traditional, well-understood *monetary* return. This is a reward, in the form of dollars, for whatever the investor "puts at risk." However, a monetary outcome is not the only dimension of the utility function.

The second kind of return consists of *social outcomes* produced by the organization receiving the resources offered by the investor. Thus, this kind of return involves identifiable social values, preferred by the investor, that have beneficial *end results* for other persons as well as for the investor—Kirk (1985).

What this theory should tell NPS organization board members and CSEs is that they are challenged to view prospective donors differently. These NPS organization leaders must find ways to bring donors into a dynamic relationship beginning with their initial gift. That relationship must be based on values and characterized by continual communication of the 'return' on their investment. The theory described in Box 5.1 presupposes an implicit belief that donors are really *donor-investors*—i.e. individuals who provide financial support for the mission of an enterprise as a means of achieving *communal benefits* that they desire.

A couple of simple illustrations may help you to understand these processes and relationships. Earlier in this chapter I mentioned the fact that I once served as treasurer of the Fund. The primary societal ERs to which that NPS organization is committed to make 'come to pass' are increases in *affordable housing opportunities* for low-income residents of the Greater Washington Area. During the time I was treasurer, the Fund had achieved less than moderate success in its participation in donor/subsidy markets. That was because the core leaders of the Fund had not demonstrated a clear and sustained connection between its output offerings and benefits for target segments of these markets.

A second illustration is also drawn from my experience of service on the board of directors of an NPS organization. As mentioned earlier in this chapter, the organization is a workforce development enterprise. Currently certain federal and state government agencies are interested in societal ERs, which they have stated as "people moved from welfare rolls into productive and permanent employment."

The enterprise offers employment and training outputs that (1) transform currently unemployable welfare recipients into employment-eligible ones and (2) place these new employment-ready individuals in permanent jobs in local business firms, government agencies, and social service organizations.

As long as the workforce development enterprise can demonstrate a direct link between its output offerings and societal benefits that particular government agencies are interested in, it will receive a flow of needed resources from them. In other words, there will continue to be mutually beneficial exchanges between the enterprise and government agencies interested in a certain kind of workforce development.

Unmistakable social, economic and political signs indicate that turbulence will continue to characterize the environments of all public-serving organizations well beyond this first decade of the twenty-first century. There are now, and there will continue to be, tremendous pressures on limited resources. The two illustrations just given should indicate that a potential donor or grantor needs a symbolic view of the performance of any given NPS organization.

I am talking about a view that has great significance beyond mere programs, projects, and activities. Potential donors and grantors need to "see" with both mind and heart the societal as well as personal values that the provision of resources for a program, project or activity will actually make "come to pass."

For an individual or group within a given segment of the donor/subsidy market, a good or service that an NPS organization offers its clients or customers represents a complex cluster of potential satisfactions. Since neither will have any direct experience with this good or service, it will not have real value per se.

In donor/subsidy markets, real value may be attached to an organization's exchanges with its clients or customers. If so, it will be in proportion to the perceived ability of these transactions to satisfy particular needs or interests that some specific individual or group has.

It is critical that board members and CSEs of NPS organizations understand that for prospective donors or grantors, the *value* of any transaction the organizations have with a client or customer resides only in the *vicarious* benefits that the potential benefactors perceive or desire. These vicarious benefits are associated with particular social-impact goals of benefactors.

Human beings are, and always have been diversely motivated beings. We act instrumentally, but also noninstrumentally. We act for material gain, but also for psychological well-being and gratification, and for social connectedness. There is nothing new or earth shattering about this...(Yochai Benkler, 2006, 6).

The recent philanthropic gifts of Bill Gates, Warren Buffett and Bon Jovi are dramatic illustrations of the fundamental principle discussed here. In the context of our discussion, the large amount or size of their gifts is not the most relevant consideration. What is extraordinarily relevant is the fact that each of these high-profile SEinvestors wants the grantee organizations to make positive and identifiable differences in the life circumstances of real people.

One final comment should be made before concluding this section on the marketing functions of an NPS organization's board of directors. Under the pressure of declining governmental revenues and fierce competition for private sector dollars, a large number of NPS organizations have opted for partial commercialization of some of their existing projects. Others are establishing subsidiary commercial enterprises that they will conduct in addition to their noncommercial programs The idea is to use any net income from commercially run enterprises to help subsidize the NPS organization's other operation.

Under certain circumstances, this resource mobilization strategy may offer significant benefits for the organization. However, as a general rule, the board of directors should not authorize it without first thoroughly and systematically analyzing and addressing the challenges it presents. The board must understand the major regulatory issues involved and make sure that the organization is capable of effectively dealing with them. Commercial production and delivery of some goods and services will add another dimension to the board's marketing functions. The board will have to exercise diligence to ensure that commercialization of some of its operations does not negatively impact the public-interest commitments of the NPS organization or erode its overall ethical standards and values. (Cf. Shore, 1999 and 1995; also Emerson and Twersky, 1996.)

In my view (1) if the board fulfills its trusteeship obligations (see Chapter1), (2) if it appropriately monitors executive management (see Chapter 2), (3) if it fosters Triple L Commitments (See Chapter 3), and (4) if it carries out its evaluation responsibilities, which we will discuss in Chapter 7—then the board will be able to make prudent decisions regarding commercialization of any of the NPS organization's operations.

This is not to say that all such prudent board decisions will satisfy those who appear to have a view of some state of affairs, which they commonly characterize as unadulterated 'nonprofitness.' Nevertheless I believe it will be generally acceptable to apply a "prudent decision" rule regarding commercialization of any of the NPS organization's operations, as long as the board of directors remains faithful to the basic public interest commitments of the organization. Ultimately, the purpose of the NPS organization is to make positive differences in the lives of real people and in the quality of life of communities. The "community-wealth" movement is showing that NPS organizations may properly depart radically "from deeply ingrained practices that have constrained those working on behalf of the public interest. ...[They may draw] upon the most powerful incentives of the marketplace and bend them toward specific community purposes instead of personal enrichment" (Shore, 1999, 304).

Ensuring Proper Use of Resources

Seeing that public-interest commitments are aligned with real needs of society, and ensuring the availability of resources to carry out these commitments, are not enough. It is also important that an organization uses its resources properly.

Therefore, there is a third and final dimension of a board's role in equipping an NPS organization for work. It is making sure that the organization's resources are used in effective, efficient, and responsible ways.

In the context of this discussion, effectiveness may be viewed as fulfilling an organization's choices of ERs. It is the relationship between organization outputs and choices of ERs. A board's duty includes seeing that all uses of resources are intentionally directed to translating these choices into reality. Ensuring that resources are used effectively means, therefore, having them deployed in ways that will make happen the end conditions, the states of affairs, and the relationships among people, things and institutions that the board wants to "come to pass" (Kirk 1986, 50).

A couple of examples will illustrate the point. Let's again take the case of the workforce development NPS enterprise. The board performs the role under review here when it ensures that resources are used (a) to make currently unemployable welfare recipients employable and (b) to place them in productive and permanent jobs. You will recall that this is what the choices of ERs of this NPS organization are all about.

Similarly, the board of the Fund ensures effective use of that NPS organization's resources by seeing that an increase in affordable housing for low-income persons actually occurs in the Greater Washington Area. The choices of ERs of the Fund are expressed in these terms. Programming is conducted and resources are allocated on this basis.

Ensuring efficiency in the use of an organization's resources involves a different emphasis. It means seeing that the organization does not use resources unnecessarily in implementing chosen ERs. Efficiency is measured by the amount of output (goods and services) produced per unit of input (i.e., dollars, person hours of staff time, etc.). Stated another way, efficiency involves getting maximum ERs from the use of a given amount of resources.

To see that an organization is equipped for efficient performance is a responsibility of its governing board. The board may not lawfully abdicate its legal authority and duty to ensure that the organization does not waste publicly contributed resources (Oleck 1988, 745).

Traditionalists in the field of organization theory would probably end our discussion at this point. That is because the scope of their immediate concerns rarely goes beyond issues of effectiveness and efficiency. However, the paradigm shift represented in this book compels me to recognize *responsibleness* as an aspect of the proper use of organization resources.

Chapter 2 discussed 'responsibleness' from the perspective of managing the managers, in a board's performance of trusteeship duties. Much of what I said there applies here, although the context is the board's duty to equip an organization for work.

Effectiveness and efficiency principles generally assume that the use of organization resources can be explained from a practical viewpoint—hat is, in terms such as productivity, feasibility, economy, and cost-benefit ratios. In contrast, responsibleness goes beyond practicality. It introduces ethical and moral perspectives. The use of an organization's resources is therefore also appraised according to ethical values and principles such as fairness, equity, equality, freedom, truthfulness, privacy, and human dignity.

In equipping an NPS organization for work, the board has a duty to see that uses of resources are consistent with generally accepted ethical and moral standards of the communities in which the organization operates.

In the preceding paragraph, I cautiously chose the words 'generally accepted.' As indicated earlier in the section of this chapter that discusses stakeholder expectations, I know that all large communities are diverse and pluralistic in their make up. The consequence of this variety is that often there are divergent and at times conflicting views, in particular settings, regarding what constitutes responsible uses of organization resources. These situations may present board members with complex dilemmas. Nevertheless, in most communities one can find broad areas of common agreement on what is an ethically acceptable or unacceptable use of the resources of an NPS organization.

The point of emphasis here is a principle that is quite simple. Neither effectiveness nor efficiency, or any combination of the two, can be regarded as an absolute standard for resource use in every conceivable situation. For example, neither effectiveness nor efficiency considerations, alone or conjointly, justify using organization resources in ways that violate law, or create serious community health problems, or pose a threat to the safety of the local populace.

In my experience, there has been and continues to be one area in which NPS organizations can hardly consistently claim exemplary performance. It is in the use of their human resources.

Boards of directors of NPS organizations are not noted for insisting on adherence to the *socially responsible* personnel policies and practices that their members often fervently advocate for commercially managed business enterprises.

Boards appear all too frequently to believe that an organization's not-for-profit status excuses socially irresponsible uses of human resources. The major premises that prior sections of this chapter and previous chapters of this book have espoused should indicate quite clearly that I do not share such a perspective on the so-called 'non-profit organization.'

What Does the Board Need?

We have examined three basic tasks of boards of directors that involve equipping NPS organizations for work. As presented here, they are:

1. Ensuring that the public-interest commitments of an NPS organization are focused on important societal issues and problems.

2. Ensuring that an NPS organization obtains the resources for the programs its public-interest commitments require.

3. Ensuring that the resources of an NPS organization are used properly.

A relevant question to ask is "What does an NPS organization board itself need in order to be able to perform these three tasks effectively, efficiently and responsibly?"

To fully answer this question would take us farther into a how-to-do-it discussion than the design of this book accommodates. It will suffice to end the discussion of Chapter 5 by simply highlighting several major needs of boards of directors of NPS organizations.

First, and by far the most urgent need is a critical mass of directors who accept, without any mental reservation, the essential premise that ultimately it is the board's duty to adequately resource an organization. This duty is part of the job description of the *office* of board director. A person is irresponsible, to say the least, if he or she accepts a directorship without accepting this duty, which a directorship entails. And the board itself behaves irresponsibly if it approves a nomination without seriously discussing this duty with the person involved.

Second, a board needs a competent, dedicated, and creative group of officers. As noted earlier in this chapter, the board officer group sets the tone and controlling examples for the rest of the directors. In the matter of ensuring adequate resourcing of the organization, as in all other matters, the ability and performance of the board as a whole cannot regularly rise above that of the board officer group. If board officers as a group fail to take "responsible charge" (Mueller 1977, 29) of equipping an NPS organization for work, the consequence is that the organization is not likely to possess, on an ongoing basis, the "capacity to survive a blow, to adapt to sudden change, and to avail itself of new opportunities" (Drucker 1980, 1).

Third, a board needs a balanced, entrepreneurial, and ERs-oriented executive committee. The reason for this has been cogently explained as follows by one author:

> An "executive committee"...comprises an advisory group, which works with top management to review and advise on major organizational issues. Members meet more frequently than the full board and act as a backup to the management. But because they represent the longer-term interest of the organization, they have a separable and often wider perspective than the managers. They are in effect the link between the overall governance role and the managers' decision-making regarding policy interpretation at the highest operating level of the organization. This link is a functional one that is necessary regardless of the size of an organization.... Thus, for a board to be most productive in its work of governance, in most instances, it will need to have the equivalent of an executive committee (Leon Haller, 1982, 167).

I have been able to draw one simple but straightforward and very important conclusion from the experiences of the many NPS organizations with which I have worked. If a board does not have an executive committee that actually expands and supplements the leadership of the organization's officer group, then the overall performance of the board in equipping the organization for work is generally unsatisfactory.

Fourth, to effectively, efficiently and responsibly perform the role of equipping an NPS organization for work, a board needs to establish and maintain good systems and processes for making resource allocation decisions. In some situations the board may be able to rely on the procedures used by staff executives in formulating their resource allocation recommendations. However, in most instances board members are likely to find that responsible board decision-making requires going beyond these staff procedures.

For example, it is unusual in NPS organizations to find staff executives or top managers who link budgeting (resource allocation) to programming (deciding on outputs and ERs to be produced). Yet unless a decision allocating money and other resources is related to outputs and chosen ERs for a given time period, that decision fails to meet the minimum standard of responsible decision-making. A board, therefore, needs to address this issue in its CSE job design, which is discussed in Chapter 2 of this book.

Most important...is the need to make sure strategic thinking precedes, rather than follows, budgeting. Unfortunately, the only strategic plans most organizations have are their budgets, and those budgets typically have been formulated without benefit of any strategic thought. Attention to mission, mandates, situational assessments, and strategic issues should precede development of budgets (Bryson, 1988, 181).

Fifth, a board needs good linkage or networking systems and processes, and a sound evaluation program. These matters are the main subjects Chapters 6 and 7.

Finally, the board and staff leaders of NPS organizations need to "put away the tin cup and go beyond fund raising" (Grace 1997, ix-x) to:

- Positioning the organization as one that meets needs, not as an organization that has needs;
- Focusing on program End Results, not just on financial goals;
- Remembering that the process of asking and giving is based in shared values;
- Engaging organization leaders and donors at all levels in a process that will convert them to donor-investors, committed to long-term relationships based on shared values and vision;
- Positioning all contributions to the organization as investments in the communities the organization serves; and

- Seeing the activities of (a) revenue generation and (b) constituency involvement as much larger, more inclusive, and energizing processes called *development.*

Next Chapter

Thus far in this book I have emphasized that performing the roles of (1) trusteeship, (2) managing the managers, (3) facilitating a learning organization, (4) serving as a catalyst and (5) equipping an NPS organization for work necessarily occurs in an environment populated by many stakeholders. Both individuals and collectives are important stakeholders.

Effective, efficient and responsible governance and management of NPS organizations in turbulent stakeholder environments also involves establishing and maintaining various kinds of linkages. Chapter 6 is devoted to a discussion of roles and responsibilities of boards with respect to creating and sustaining linkage relationships.

Chapter 6

Establishing and Maintaining Linkages

Organization as we know it is obsolete in the information society in which we now exist. Those of us in management who weave human networks have confounded both ourselves and our establishments. These human networks are thriving while the organizations around them struggle to be effective—or even to survive. There seems to be an intuitive notion that somehow, someway, networking may be basic to organizing and managing people in the future. Robert K. Mueller, *Corporate Networking,* 1986.

Today the strategic challenge of doing more with less leads corporations to look outward as well as inward for solutions to the competitiveness dilemma, improving their ability to compete without adding internal capacity... They can pool resources with others, to exploit opportunity, or link systems in a partnership. Rosabeth M. Kanter, *When Giants Learn To Dance,* 1989.

Fifty-three years ago our attention was interestingly called to the fact that we were then—and we still are—n the midst of an 'organizational revolution' (Boulding 1953).

Fifteen years later we were informed that our society had become a 'society of organizations' (Drucker 1968). More recently, we have been told that we live in an "organizationally rich" society, and that "the environment of any one organization is composed of many other organizations" (Kast and Rosenweig (1979).

This latter characterization of our society is very important. It poses some critical challenges for the species of organization that is the subject of this book. It means that all organizations comprising that species need to pursue a carefully designed strategy of productively interacting with the other entities in the "organizationally rich" society.

You will recall that the type of organization we are talking about is referred to in this book as the nongovernmental public-serving (NPS) organization. This book advances the proposition that one set of roles of board members involves responsibilities with respect to the formulation and implementation of strategies governing interactions of their NPS organizations with other entities.

It is the objective of Chapter 6 to identify and describe some of these responsibilities. As the chapter title suggests, we view them in terms of establishing and maintaining linkages between an NPS organization and other enterprises in its local polity.

Linkages

The fact that an NPS organization operates in an organizationally rich society means that it must achieve and sustain some level of cooperation and support from other entities. Securing essential cooperation and support depends largely on the ongoing patterns of inter-organization relationships that exist.

Current literature contains an array of terms as descriptors of inter-organization relationships. The terms used include affiliation, alliance, joint ventures, network, partnership, and merger. Here, for the purposes of this book, we use the phrase inter-organization linkage as a generic term to refer to any formalized arrangement or mechanism under which two or more 'free-standing' organizations may engage in collaborative undertakings or productive behaviors.

In a substantial part of the literature, inter-organization linkages are commonly viewed as part of a comprehensive strategy of resource control. We could have easily discussed linkages in the previous chapter. However, we intentionally chose not to do so. The reason is that in any NPS organization there are additional important considerations. For example, in some situations certain types of linkages have crucial implications for the legitimacy of particular NPS organizations.

In the governance context of this book inter-organization linkages refer to formal or official collaboration between an NPS organization and one or more other entities in the environment of the NPS enterprise. More generally, inter-organization linkages are formally expressed inter-dependencies among public-serving organizations that affect performance of the mission of each.

In each instance of inter-organizational linkage, organizations become bounded together through interpenetration of personnel, as in the case of executive movement or interlocking directorates, or through a pooling of assets, as in the case of joint ventures (Pfeffer 1987, 146).

The devices that any NPS organization may use to forge particular inter-organization linkages are many and varied. At the governance level, a special structural linkage mechanism is associated with governmentally mandated diversity in the composition of the governing boards of some NPS organizations. This governmental strategy is traceable to the social activism of the 1960s.

In August of 1964, congress enacted and the president signed the Economic Opportunity Act of 1964 (EOA). Title II of the EOA established a federal "community action" program. Under it local NPS organizations called community action agencies (CAAs), had to have a tripartite board structure in order to qualify for federal grants. One-third of the board members had to be local government officials or their designees; one-third had to be *representatives* of the primary beneficiaries of the program; and the other third could be chosen from business, labor, religious, educational, and social welfare organizations.

Thus, forty-two years ago a federal program initiated a policy of forging linkages at the board level of certain NPS organizations that received government support. The policy is still in vogue today.

It can be illustrated here by referring to the workforce development enterprise discussed in the previous chapter of this book. As an NPS organization, it has linkages with the county government. The board of directors of the enterprise includes members appointed by the County Executive. Also included on the board are representatives of other institutions such as business, education, civic groups, labor, and social welfare organizations. This pattern of diversity in board composition is required for eligibility to receive grants under the federal Workforce Investment Act.

This example shows the possibility that any particular NPS organization may have several different types of inter-organization linkages with a variety of other enterprises. Directors are quite often the means of achieving these linkages. In effect, board members become what the Likerts (1976) refer to as "link-ing persons." They are expected to be channels of productive communication and collaboration between the NPS organization and certain specific stakeholder groups in the organization's environment.

We should note that frequently an opposite or reverse process is in opera-tion. Board members of NPS organizations are appointed to serve on governing bodies of other public-serving enterprises as their organizations' *representatives.* The author has noted elsewhere (Kirk 1986, 167-171) that these types of repre-sentation can cause delicate problems of governance as well as produce benefits for the NPS organization. In such linkages a critical aspect of the board's job is "the management of relations rather than...the management of discrete ac-tivities" (Morgan 1988, 130). With respect to community action programs of the 1960s, much of the "maximum feasible misunderstanding" scorned by Moyni-han (1969) was caused by attempts of boards of directors to control linkage ac-tivities rather than to manage relationships.

Obviously, the board of an NPS organization may employ inter-organiza-tion linkage mechanisms to help it obtain necessary resources for the enterprise. Some boards have achieved a significant degree of success in using these mechanisms for resource mobilization purposes. Perhaps most notable among them, at the local community level, appears to be museum, symphony, art, thea-ter, and sheltered workshop enterprises. Regionally and nationally, institutions of higher education and hospitals or other health care providers have been quite successful using this approach.

The interlocking directorate is not the only available inter-organization linkage mechanism. Other collaborative devices include joint ventures, inte-grated service alliances, partnerships, and shared facilities and personnel. A joint venture is a contractual relationship between an NPS organization and one or more other enterprises to carry out some specific undertaking.

It is important to note that in all of these forms of collaboration, the corpo-rate or legal entity of the NPS organization will remain in existence. "This is the business structure that has an official purpose, a board of directors, officers, by-laws, and all those other things generally recognized to be part of overseeing a corporate body" (McLaughlin 1998, 54).

Boards of directors and chief staff executives (CSEs) may consider a joint venture a less risky or a less expensive way of initiating some new undertaking. For example, a board might consider this type of linkage where an organization has the technology for a given undertaking but lacks the financial resources or marketing skills. Joint ventures are not necessarily problem free. They may work out badly if the collaborating organizations have different corporate stakes that lead to inconsistent demands on their governing and managing systems and processes.

In integrated service alliances, a group of NPS organizations and other public-serving entities with a similar need ban together to create a new enterprise to fill that need for all of them. The service is one that is too expensive or difficult for a single organization to provide for itself, and there are insurmountable obstacles to obtaining it on the open market. So several organizations collaborate to create a new organization, which they jointly control, to meet the need. An example of this type of linkage in the Greater Washington, DC area is the Center for Nonprofit Advancement (CNA). CNA is an instrument of over thirty public-serving organizations. It provides insurance, accounting, and purchasing services for its member organizations. In Maryland, the Maryland Association of Nonprofit Organizations (MANO) provides similar services for its organizational members.

As viewed here, partnerships have some features that are similar to those of joint ventures. But they also show significant differences. The critical difference is that partnerships have a longer time span and they involve important aspects of the ongoing operations of the NPS organization. In other words, partnerships have a program focus while joint ventures are usually project oriented and time specific. Driven by financial necessity, in recent years more and more NPS organizations are forging partnerships that can generate income to help meet their budget needs. (See Crimmins and Keil 1983; Grace 1997; and Sagawa and Segal 2000.) To some degree this development is fueled by the incentives of 'contracting out' and other forms of the 'privatization' movement. (See Salamon 1995 and Donahue 1989.)

The sharing of personnel, facilities, and equipment is another manifestation of the use of inter-organization linkage mechanisms. Cases of this form of sharing have become more numerous among NPS organizations as a consequence of the "Reagan Revolution" and its aftermath. The author has recently served as a consultant to organizations that shared a personnel specialist, an accountant, and a program planner. All of the organizations involved occupied the same building—two were on the same floor of the building. It is no longer an uncommon phenomenon to find small NPS organizations sharing computers and computer time.

Both business and social sector organizations are reinventing themselves by forming alliances. In both sectors, partnerships have been a way to expand capabilities beyond what the organization's own resource base permits. Alliances allow organizations greater flexibility and the opportunity to leverage competencies, improve customer service, and create a wider geographic reach (Sagawa and Segal, 2000, 7).

The discussion up to this point should be sufficient to clearly indicate that inter-organization linkages are formal or structured arrangements. They are mutually beneficial for all organizations involved. In some cases they enable these organizations to accomplish common objectives collaboratively. However, before we elaborate further on specific linkage roles for board members, we should briefly discuss what is involved in more informal interactions between public-serving organizations.

Networks and Networking

The idea of networks between organizations, and the notion of networking by organizations, are relatively new concepts. We tend to associate networking phenomena primarily as particular aspects of interactions among individuals. Thus it is common to hear people talk about the 'old-boys network.' The reference is to systems of interrelationships among males presumed to have positive effects on their careers. In this individual context, 'networking' is actions and activities aimed at building such systems of interrelationships. These behaviors by individuals may occur within and across boundaries of organizations.

This chapter emphasizes board roles and responsibilities that go beyond networks or networking aimed at personal advancement. Here we are concerned with application of these concepts to behaviors of organizations that result from board leadership. This is the context in which we focus on both networks and networking.

Unfortunately, there is no one definition of the term network that commands universal acceptance. The term means different things to different people. The same individuals, when considering the term in varying contexts, often emphasize different connotations of networks.

A generally useful definition of networks views them as configurations of different entities in which decision-making "is no longer part of some hierarchy but is shared among autonomous units" (Hage, 1998).

Using terminology and phraseology quite liberally from the works of Lipnack and Stamps (1982), Mueller says various experts on the subject view networks as

> informal systems...The nature of networks is that they are short-lived, self-camouflaging...adisciplinary...invisible, uncountable, unpollable, and may be active or inactive. In practical terms, networks feature spontaneous feedback via telephone, mail, meetings, computers, or a shout across the room, if this is possible (Mueller, 1986, 21).

Informality seems to be one commonly acknowledged characteristic of networks (Nohria and Eccles 1992). This conclusion appears to be supported by Nancy Foy in her statement of the "purpose" and the "law" of a network:

> Time purpose of a network is the flow of informal information.... Informal networks are particularly effective for the flow of informal information because they create windows in organizational wall, without damaging the sense of membership of people inside those walls... The effectiveness of a network is inversely proportional to its informality (Foy, 1980).

The descriptions of Foy, and the conclusory statement of Mueller presented earlier in the chapter, should suffice as an articulation of a broad theory of networks and networking. Our interest here is in applying this framework to NPS organizations. More specifically, it is to examine roles and responsibilities of boards of directors that involve creating networks and engaging in networking processes of behalf of such organizations.

Why Organization Linkages and Networks?

In prior sections of this chapter we articulated our definitions of the following terms

- *Inter-organization linkages* are formal or official collaborative connections between a particular organization and one or more other entities in its environment.

- *Organization networks* are informal patterns of interaction between governing and managing officials of organizations in which participants informally exchange information, and receive what they perceive as acceptable levels of benefits or support for the organization they govern or manage.

In the context of those definitions I pose the following two-part question: Is it absolutely essential that the governing and managerial processes of any NPS organization include such linkages and networks? Should an NPS organization create and sustain inter-organization linkages, and participate strategically in organization networks?

My answer to both parts of the question is an unequivocal "yes." Why the "yes" answers?

In answering "yes" I recognize that most NPS organizations appear positioned to respond reasonably well to new needs for managerial innovation. In relatively recent times foundations and governmental funding sources have given increased attention to improving the quality of top management. But in my view the typical NPS organization is ill equipped to respond satisfactorily to new emerging needs for innovations in *governance* concepts and procedures.

The fact is that today and in the future NPS organizations are not likely to acquire and sustain the needed capability for innovative governance without forging the kinds of inter-organizational linkages and networks that I have briefly discussed here.

Absent such inter-organizational relationships—within the boardroom, for example—the long-term ability of an NPS enterprise's board to successfully ensure the achievement of the enterprise's public-interest commitments will be problematical. The board of directors cannot be certain that the enterprise will have the organizational capability required to effectively achieve the End Results (ERs) the board has chosen. This means that the legitimacy of the NPS organization may be jeopardized. (See Chapter 1 of this book.)

To some readers of this book my assessment of the current situation may seem unrealistic. If that is the case, then consider the crucial and wide-ranging implications for NPS organizations of the assessment of McLaughlin, which is presented in Box 6.1.

> **Box 6.1**
>
> Today, we are in the very beginning stages of what promises to be the single largest restructuring of our system of service delivery in history. It is reaching across sectors, from hospitals and social service agencies to associations and cultural groups...[T]his restructuring is privately initiated and privately managed. It goes by code names such as managed care, capitated payments, block grants, and program-related investments...
>
> [T]he focus of innovation in the nonprofit sector has shifted. In the last two or three decades, innovation occurred in the delivery of services. Terms such as community residences, outreach programs and supported employment that are commonplace today were revolutionary program innovations as recently as the 1960s.
>
> The bulk of innovation today will take place not in programs and services but in management. And the thrust of that innovation will be toward greater collaboration between nonprofit organizations and all others carrying out similar missions. What we call mergers and alliances are really just a part of the innovation that the nonprofit sector must deliver over the next two or three decades. —McLaughlin (1998, xxi-xxii).

One of the epigraphs at the beginning of this chapter is from Rosabeth Kanter's *When Giants Learn To Dance*. The "giants" Kanter refers to are large, complex and commercially run organizations. Kanter uses the word "dance" allegorically to symbolize these organizations' desperate need for creativity, adaptability, flexibility and agility. She suggests that by adopting a strategy of "becoming PALS," that is, *pooling, allying* and *linking*, the giants will learn to dance.

This book explicitly acknowledges that not all NPS organizations are large. However, it strongly argues that all of them are unavoidably located in highly complex environments. They, too, must learn how to dance. In the process of becoming 'learning organizations' all NPS enterprises must learn:

- How to engage in mutual exchanges of information.
- How to pool resources with others.
- How to create alliances to exploit opportunities.
- How to link systems in partnerships.
- How to participate in joint ventures.
- How to form consortia.

- How to take partial ownership positions that significantly contribute to fulfillment of their public-interest commitments.

Every passing day yields more plausible evidence that the future environment of most NPS organizations will contain many entities that are "a network of various contracted relationships, joint ventures, partial ownership positions, and other strategic alliances" (Gailbraith and Kazanjian, 1988). In order to remain viable in the future, an NPS organization must be able to interact effectively with these emerging non-traditional kinds of entities.

An example of a new nontraditional entity readily comes to mind. It is the approach to school-business-community partnerships that is being used in several localities throughout the United States. Entities generically called *community holding companies* (i.e. special kinds of NPS organizations) are being established to administer these partnerships. Such holding companies have created project offices to actually administer partnerships between the school system, business enterprises, local governments, and social service institutions. Many of these holding companies are funded by commercially run organizations. Thus, key business, government, school-system and other community leaders have networked to form organizations of considerable adaptability, flexibility, and creativity.

Generally speaking, day-to-day core project office operations of the holding company are funded from nongovernmental sources, or staffed by volunteers from the community. As a specific project is identified for implementation, it is then funded individually, with resources coming from all available sources.

The device of a community holding company is not intended to compete with existing public-serving organizations but rather to work with them. It may also serve as an instrument for coordinating the contributions of a variety of organizations.

The urgent need for governing boards of NPS organizations to perform leadership roles with respect to critical inter-organizational relationships is not generally recognized or explicitly acknowledged. In written and oral discussions of such relationships predominant emphasis is focused elsewhere. It centers on staff responsibilities, particularly those of the CSE.

This book goes against the grain of much conventional wisdom. Its message is that in the NPS organization, there are 'organizational-linking' and 'organizational-networking' functions that staff executives cannot perform effectively. Moreover, there are others that they should perform rarely, if at all. For instance, I have observed situations where great damage to NPS organizations has occurred from boards' exclusive reliance on staff executives to perform delicate networking tasks involving important elected officials of local polities.

At a minimum, the officers of a board must be sufficiently perceptive to recognize when it is inappropriate for staff executives to assume leadership roles in building inter-organization linkages or networks that necessarily involve the domain of governance. Recently published reports about serious survival threats to well-known public-serving organizations should underscore the reality of this book's message.

In any case, the primary emphasis here is that every NPS organization exists in an environment that is composed of a multiplicity of other entities. Patterns of relationships among all of them are dynamic. They are constantly changing. As noted above in Box 6-1, new and more complex modes of interaction are emerging in this first decade of the twenty-first century. This development is largely a consequence of the ongoing revolution in communications, information processing, transportation, and other technologies that make our world a global village. An NPS organization is not likely to be a viable enterprise within the polity in which it operates without building and maintaining inter-organization linkages and networks.

There is only one major remaining issue for us to address in this chapter. It is to explain (1) why this vital process is not confined to the domain of management, (2) why the board of directors must play a leadership role in ongoing interaction between the organization and key stakeholder institutions and (3) why the function of governance comes to center stage so prominently.

This most critical issue involves

- Legitimacy considerations;
- Political factors;
- Viability of public-interest commitments;
- Resourcing strategies; and
- Keeping the organization geared to the future.

Brief comments on each of these issues will follow immediately.

Legitimacy

In Chapter 1 of this book we said that ensuring the legitimacy of an NPS organization is a very important aspect of the governing board's trusteeship roles. A board cannot fulfill this obligation in the long term without exercising effective leadership with respect to inter-organization linkages and organization networks.

Chapters 1 and 5 explained that legitimacy refers to particular perceptions of and beliefs about an organization. In other words, legitimacy is an impression in the minds and hearts of people—as individuals and as participants in other social units—that *this NPS organization is good*, or that *it has a rightful place in our community*.

Another way to verbalize this belief and feeling is to do so in language very much in use today by executives of government and commercially run enterprises. For example, an NPS organization may be said to have legitimacy if people can say that it is 'socially responsible' or that it fulfills 'its ethical responsibilities to society.'

When a board thinks about linkages and networks, in relation to legitimacy, it needs to keep in mind that the local polity in which any NPS organization exists is not composed simply of two big divisions. That is, those who view the organization as legitimate and those who believe it is not legitimate. Rather, the local polity is much more complex than that. It includes various subgroups. Each perceives, believes, and acts differently toward the organization.

A board needs to ensure the establishment of organization-linkages and the building of organization-networks reflective of the reality that each subgroup has a mental image of its own relationship to the NPS organization.

A board will find that the various subgroups may be arranged along a continuum. At one end are support subgroups. They are composed of individuals and collectives that actively support the organization by providing resources, including *political capital*. At the other end are opposition subgroups. Included in these subgroups are persons who, in extreme cases, deny that the organization has a legitimate right to continue its operations. They can be broken down into external opponents and internal opponents.

In the middle are two other types of identifiable subgroups. Nearer the 'support' end of the continuum are subgroups that passively signify their approval of the NPS organization. They consist of a cluster of persons who, though not actively supporting the organization, nevertheless feel that it is good, and that it has a legitimate place in the local polity. These persons range all the way from those who take pride in having the organization as part of the local polity to those who have a nonspecific belief that the organization may some day do them some good.

When the board of directors of an NPS organization considers these four types of subgroups it should easily realize that the support and approval ones have positive legitimacy images of the organization for various reasons. Their images derive partly from the functional significance of the organization's public-interest commitments, and partly from existing organization-linkages and organization-networks.

The kinds of linkage and networking strategies that the board needs to nurture should be clearly obvious. They are strategies aimed at (a) expanding the clusters of *support* and *approval* subgroups, (b) reducing the *opposition* subgroups, and (c) converting *indifference* subgroups into support and approval ones.

It is certainly true that the team of executive managers shares important responsibility with the board in connection with any design and implementation of such strategies. However, irreparable damage to the legitimacy of an organization may occur if the board fails to perform its roles or abdicates its responsibility with respect to creating and sustaining critical linkages and vital networks.

Political Factors

All linking and networking relationships that an NPS organization may develop with other public-serving entities in the local polity in which it operates will, unavoidably, have some political aspects. (You will recall that Chapter 5 defined 'political' non-pejoratively as decisions and actions aimed at influencing the distribution of finite societal utilities where there are common, sometimes overlapping, and often-conflicting claims.)

In turbulent environments, there will be an increasing number of instances where the political dimensions will be substantial and critical. Strategic leadership in fostering linkages and networks in such environments needs to emanate from the boardroom of an NPS organization.

As an example, it seems plausible that board officers should take the lead in negotiating organization-linkages with local governments that require annual appropriations support from the city council or other local legislative body.

Yet, my consulting services were utilized in one instance where the CSE and staff managers got an organization in great difficulty. The CSE initiated the process of forming such a linkage without the necessary political networking by governing board members. The mayor of the city involved viewed the initiative of the CSE negatively—as part of a broader plan of the staff to position the CSE to run for elective office in the local government. Consequently, the mayor vetoed the appropriations act.

In previous chapters of this book we have indicated our view that the word political is not necessarily a dirty word. And we also do not believe that it must always suggest a negative concept. Thus, in the particular setting of an NPS organization, that which is political pertains to issues, processes or actions involving attempts by one person/group to influence others to behave in ways preferred by the first person/group.

In order for an organization's board to establish and sustain certain organization-linkages and organization-networks with other entities, it must have what Harris (1985, 14) calls "political savvy—the ability to identify, then gain support and agreement from, various constituencies or governmental actors/entities."

In working with governing boards, it has been my experience that if they lack political savvy, they simply cannot meet the most strategic needs of NPS organizations at crucial times or in critical situations. Many NPS organizations, under the influence of multiple contracts, subcontracts, and project grants, have in fact become components of loosely structured but complex network systems. Through these systems a lot of social services are being delivered to targeted segments of urban and rural polities.

Effective and responsible governance of all entities involved in these network systems requires (1) a new sense of collective identity, (2) managerial philosophies that recognize the importance of mutual dependence and collaboration, and (3) a collective sense of accountability and control.

Every NPS organization is probably associated with some network system. Those that have officers who lack political savvy are not likely to serve the organization very well, with respect to performing linkage and networking roles. For in such network systems, as Morgan (1988, 130) observes, "interorganizational relations become as important as intraorganizational relations." Great political skill is required to manage inter-organizational relations. This is especially the case where interorganizational network relationships are impacted by different policy and program requirements of two or more governmental funding sources.

Typically, there are competing interests between different governmental funding agencies, and these competing interests give rise to conflict in the form of persistent bureaucratic politics. It is crucial that NPS governing boards have well conceived strategies for dealing with the inter-bureaucratic conflicts of the

different governmental agencies from which they get financial and other support. Yates views all managers as "political detectives" (1985, 59-89). I also
view the leaders of boards of directors of NPS organizations as *political detectives*.

Viability of Public-Interest Commitments

In this book, we have presented the concept *public-interest commitments* as a
conceptual framework for thinking about, organizing, and conducting programmatic activities of public-serving enterprises. Viewed as societal outcomes
to be produced by an NPS organization, public-interest commitments are indicators of the usefulness of the organization to the local polity in which it exists.
But that subject is not our primary concern here. We dealt with it extensively in
Chapters 1,4 and 5.

The relevant point of emphasis in the present discussion is different. It is
that in turbulent environments, the long-term viability of an organization's public-interest commitments can best be ensured through organization-linkage and
organization-network relationships.

Generally speaking, 'viability' means having a capability of survival,
growth and development. With respect to its public-interest commitments, viability of an NPS organization involves connections to linkage/network systems
that strongly support the fulfillment of those commitments. In carrying out its
public-interest commitments, an NPS organization's implementation procedures
may encompass constantly changing functions that are linked together into dynamic networks. "Many of these functions will need to be linked to external
functions outside the traditional boundaries of the organization" (Primozic and
Leben, 1991, 213).

Gone are the days, if ever they existed, that an NPS organization's board of
directors and staff executives could accomplish the enterprise's public-interest
commitments by concentrating exclusively on effectiveness and efficiency of internal processes and systems. As indicated earlier, NPS organizations are increasingly being drawn into inter-organizational arrangements that constitute "a
network of various contracted relationships, joint ventures, partial ownership positions, and other strategic alliances" (Galbraith and Kazanjian 1988, 38).

At any given moment in every local polity, there is a set of prevailing patterns of inter-organization linkages/networks. This set is never static. It changes
over time. New institutional arrangements, like the community holding com-

pany discussed earlier, or non-proprietary charter schools, come into being. This change process always impacts NPS organizations.

In dealing with fundamental changes in community-wide organization-linkage and organization-network mechanisms, creative leadership from the boardroom is necessary in order to ensure the long-term viability of any NPS organization's public-commitments.

Development Strategies

The discussion in Chapter 5 of resourcing an NPS organization presupposed, without explicitly saying so, that resource mobilization roles of the board are an integral part of a larger paradigm of development. In this paradigm, we view resource providers as *socio-economic investors* (SEinvestors[TM]) in the mission, in the public-interest commitments and in the choices of End Results (ERs) of an NPS organization.

SEinvestors make such types of investments primarily on the basis of shared values. They see the defined communal benefits that an NPS organization is actually producing. Those benefits have some significant value for SEinvestors. In this context, development strategies aim to uncover shared values. They include identification, nurturing, and reinforcement of shared values.

Performing both individual and organizational linking/networking roles is driven by the importance of providing potential and current SEinvestors with opportunities to explore and apply these values on behalf of an NPS organization.

Here *development* presumes that all provisions of resources for the NPS organization are a form of SEinvestment, with one type of return consisting of the knowledge that values shared by both the organization and the SEinvestor are being realized. Cf. Mansbridge (1998, 13–14) for a discussion of the concept of "'nesting' public spirit within a return to self-interest."

We argue in this book that the governing board of the NPS organization must be strategically involved in the dynamic process of creating SEinvestors, individual and institutional resource providers who seek and receive dynamic relationships with the organization. When this process is planned and pursued as the sensitive and crucial activity it can be, then resourcing the NPS organization is m ore likely than not to be highly successful.

Finally, the board of directors of an NPS organization must be keenly aware of the fact that the type of resourcing strategy it pursues has a critical bearing on how well that strategy can be coordinated with other organization-linkage and organization-network initiatives the organization undertakes. Here the author underscores his personal belief that any board is likely to achieve greater long-term success coordinating organization-linkage and organization-network initiatives with development/marketing strategies than with fund-raising ones.

The mind-sets of *development/marketing* are those of genuine 'partnering.' The focus of genuine partnering is never **"What's in it for me?"** It's **"What's the value we're creating together?"** And **"Is the jointly created value one that we both share?"**

Maintaining A Future Perspective

Staying geared to the future is a major them of Chapter 4 of this book. There we elaborated upon two crucial propositions:

1. In the final analysis, it is ultimately the governing board that is account-able for keeping any NPS organization geared to the future; and
2. Success in performing this responsibility requires board members, indi-vidually and collectively as a body, to develop and exercise certain cognitive and behavioral competencies.

These propositions are part of Chapter 4's broader discussion of roles and responsibilities of directors to serve as a catalyst when necessary. Here our task is to suggest that organization-linkage and organization-network strategies can be combined with catalytic roles to facilitate keeping a future-oriented focus for an NPS organization.

Keeping any NPS organization geared to the future is fundamentally a mat-ter of its leaders formulating, communicating and implementing strategic visions that encompass emerging new realities.

By providing leadership with respect to organization-linkage and organiza-tion-network relationships, any board of directors will find it less difficult to formulate and communicate its visions of the organization's future.

Vision is about what a board wants the organization to be in terms of (a) public-interest commitments, (b) choices of ERs and (c) outputs, markets (both client/customer and donor/subsidy) and internal capabilities. A well thought-out vision may enable your board to utilize organization-linkage and organization-network devices as express lanes on the highways to some predetermined future state of the organization. At the very least, these devices or mechanisms can, when combined with a vision, facilitate organization learning. An NPS organization learns "whenever it acquires new capacity for behavior" (Schon 1971, 116).

As we noted in Chapter 3, steering NPS organizations successfully through environmental turbulence, and guiding them toward a healthy and productive future, requires governing boards to develop and exercise certain governing skills:

- They need to 'read' the environment and identify the changes relevant to their organizations.
- They need to approach the future proactively and govern their organizations from the 'outside in' to sustain an ongoing environmental focus and keep adjusted to new opportunities.
- They need to provide leadership and vision for all organization participants, and build commitment around key values and shared understandings.
- They need to develop organization cultures that encourage creativity, learning, and innovation.
- They need to develop the ability to mobilize key actors from different sectors of society for common attacks on shared problems.

Playing leadership roles in networking, in the creation of alliances and joint ventures, in building what Lipnack and Stamp (1993) describe as "Team-Net," and in establishing other inter-organizational relationships can contribute to a board's acquisition of these governing capabilities.

The findings of Bennis and Nanus (1985) in their book *Leaders*, and the "heroic" leadership premises of Murphy (1994) discussed in his book *Forging the Heroic Organization*, suggest the following: That effective boards use vision as an instrument to move organizations and people toward future conditions.

The message here is that a board can use organization-linkage and organization-network relationships as powerful devices—both to create new visions for the NPS organization and to transform these visions into future realities.

In human communication via computer, America has, as Hiltz and Turoff (1978) argue, become a "network nation." But there is also "another America" (Lipnack and Stamps 1982) that involves communication and interactions between and among organizations in "organizationally rich" (Kast and Rosenzweig 1979) local and regional polities.

I will close the discussion of the subject of Chapter 6 by stating my personal conviction that the future of NPS organizations, in the first decade of the twenty-first century and beyond, will be significantly affected by the ability of their boards of directors to effectively create, sustain and use unique interorganizational linkage systems. In summary, potentially beneficial reasons for inter-organizational cooperation include the following:

- To advance the public-interest commitments of the organization.
- To grow or otherwise expand the impact of the NPS organization in the polities in which it operates.
- To retrench, when necessary, without diminishing the quantity or quality of needed products and services.
- To reduce unproductive duplication of products and services.
- To create important synergies that otherwise would not exist.
- To enhance visibility and build community support for the public-interest commitments of the NPS organization.

But the board's basic responsibility does not end here. For beyond interorganization relationships lies the crucial matter of nurturing linkages with first-level stakeholders. As noted in previous chapters of the book, an NPS organization has many stakeholders—clients, customers, suppliers, government and private sector SEinvestors, and the general citizenry. Each of these types of groups may be affected by what an NPS organization does or intentionally refuses to do.

In my view, its first-level stakeholders are the persons, individually and collectively, for whose benefits continued existence of an NPS organization is justified.

Ultimately, the legitimacy of the organization has to be viewed in terms of how its overall performance affects the people who comprise its primary stakeholder group.

This is a standard by which the board of directors may assess all of its actual and prospective decisions regarding inter-organizational linkages and networks.

Next Chapter

In the turbulent environments of today and tomorrow, the future viability of an NPS organization may be more certain if its governing board ensures a continual increase in the depth of inter-organization relationships. From time to time, the board needs to appraise the quality and effectiveness of its own leadership—in building and sustaining vital organization-linkages and organization-networks; and in using these connections for the benefit of first-level stakeholders. This is an appropriate subject for examination in the following chapter.

Chapter 7 deals with the subject of evaluating overall organizational performance, which includes performance of the governing board itself.

Chapter 7

Evaluating Organizational Performance

To succeed in building organizational capacity as a resource for the social missions they believe in, boards need to build a culture that values organizational performance. At the outset, asking the right questions will be more important than having the precise answers, processes, or strategies for improving performance. A sustainable commitment to organizational performance needs to start with questions the board really cares about: What difference are we making in the lives of our community? Where could we do better? Christine Letts, William P. Ryan and Allen Grossman, *High Performance Nonprofit Organizations*, 1999, 143.

Evaluation is a systematic means of finding out how well you are doing the things you set out to do and the probable reasons for their success or failure. It is usually a deliberate, scheduled, and analytical process that seeks to accomplish specific aims. Its primary purpose is to examine systematically what you have been doing in the past, or what you are now doing, in order to improve your performance in the future. Jack Koteen, *Strategic Management in Public and Nonprofit Organizations*, 1989.

This book takes a different approach to the governance functions of organizations with a legally defined not-for-profit (LDNFP) status. It identifies a subset of such organizations, specifies seven sets of roles for their boards of directors, and lays out a conceptual model against which the roles may be analyzed and discussed.

Chapter 7 of the book covers the final set of governing board roles and responsibilities. The subset of organizations with the legally defined not-for-profit status is the nongovernmental public-serving (NPS) organization. The purpose of this chapter is to address the function of board evaluation of the overall performance of the NPS organization, including assessment of the governing board itself, as a key subunit of the organization.

There is a sense in which the set of board roles and responsibilities that this chapter covers is the most important of all. If these board roles are performed well, the board will find out how well the NPS organization is doing the things the board mandates. The board will also find out how good its own leading, guiding, directing and controlling behaviors are, in terms of their impact on overall performance of the organization.

Two foundational propositions underlie all that we have said in previous chapters of the book. They are cornerstones of the book's whole conceptual framework. And they are also critical to board roles and responsibilities with respect to evaluation. The two propositions are:

- An NPS organization exists to make **SOMETHING** happen—i.e., to produce End Results (ERs) in its external environment that have ascertainable beneficial values for society as a whole, or for broadly defined subparts of society.

- It is the *governing board* of the NPS organization that is ultimately accountable and answerable to the organization's stakeholders (a) for specifying the choice of ERs it is committed to produce and (b) for ensuring that the organization delivers on these commitments.

We have emphasized throughout the book that the governing board is a key subsystem of any NPS organization. Mueller (1984, 75) refers to the board as "the brain" of an organization. Carver (1990, 2) notes that a "governing board is as high in the structure as one can go and still be within the organizational framework. Its total authority is matched by its total accountability for all corporate activity."

This means that the process for evaluating overall performance of the NPS organization must include assessing the effectiveness and responsibleness of the board itself. We begin Chapter 7 with an examination of this critical issue.

Just as nonprofit boards assume oversight responsibilities for their organizations and evaluate their executives, they also need to take their own pulse from time to time. The challenges facing nonprofit boards today require imaginative leadership and the ability to thoughtfully examine basic organizational issues such as quality and costs. A board needs to periodically assess its leadership capacity in order to ensure that the organization is served well. An assessment that helps bring about positive and practical changes in the board as a group and in members' performance is a worthwhile investment of the board's time (Diane J. Duca, 1996, 129).

Assessing Board Performance

As a subunit of the NPS organization, the board of directors has a purpose. The board exists because of its purpose. The board develops and sustains itself in order to pursue and fulfill its purpose.

The effectiveness, efficiency and responsibleness of any particular board are difficult to assess with respect to any one of the seven role categories discussed in this book. Each of the seven sets encompasses a complex web of activities and processes. Consequently, the roles tend to be oversimplified, broadband descriptors for some dimensions of the *purpose* of the board of directors.

To be sure, criteria or standards for assessing the performance of a board of directors are incomplete and variable. But they are evolving more rapidly than board members and the general public may realize. During the past four decades, statutes, regulations, societal norms and mores, standards of moral and ethical conduct, and concepts of 'corporate social responsibility' have established a core of ascertainable reference points, benchmarks, and plumb lines. Additionally, the craftily reasoned ruling of a district court in 1974 in the Sibley Hospital case (*Stern v. Lucy Webb Hays Nat. Train. Sch. for Deacon. & M.*, 381 F.Supp. 1003), has provided some clear and generally useful judicial guidelines.

Our review of the literature on evaluation reveals the use of a wide range of varying types, models and approaches. It is not within the scope of this chapter to discuss them even briefly. It will suffice to note that our paradigm of Strategic Governance involves a less formal approach than complex quantitative evaluation models. We opt for what Stake (1979, 14) describes as "responsive evaluation." That is the approach we take here.

Our evaluation model focuses on concerns and interests of stakeholders of an NPS organization. It trades off some measurement precision in order to increase the usefulness of findings to board members, and to the organization's clients, customers, SEinvestors (as defined in Chapter 6), and the general public. Finally, it accommodates different value perspectives present in reporting the success and failure of the organization as a whole, including the governing board.

Our Strategic Governance paradigm requires a board of directors (a) to articulate a clear vision of an intended future for the NPS enterprise, (b) to define a set of choices of ERs for the organization to accomplish within specified periods of time, and (c) to formulate realistic resource requirements.

We operationalize board purpose in terms of a four-dimensional model, which allows us to establish relevant board performance indicators. The four dimensions of board purpose are (1) vision creation, (2) sustaining organizational legitimacy, (3) resource mobilization and (4) monitoring the impact of organizational output. Boards can use the model to assess their performance. The model is presented schematically below in Figure 7-1.

Figure 7-1   Board Assessment Model

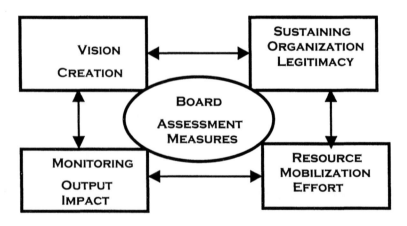

Board performance indicators may be derived from each of the four dimensions of purpose shown in Figure 7-1. For example directors can make a systematic attempt to obtain both quantitative and qualitative information that will provide them with objective answers to the following question: To what extent, if any, do board decisions and actions contribute-

(a)   To creating and sustaining a compelling vision of the organization's future—i.e., one that communicates what the organization will be and where it will go;

(b)   To continued legitimizing the organization to the local polity in which it operates;

(c)   To obtaining resources the organization needs to carry out board approved choices of ERs; and

(d)   To ensuring that the organization produces and delivers to its stakeholders outputs that fulfill its public-interest commitments?

If the directors are seriously interested in assessing the overall performance of the enterprise, then a board self-appraisal is probably the place to begin. By 'seriously interested' we mean a willingness to assemble, analyze and draw relevant conclusions from pertinent data regarding board behaviors.

Directors can organize such data around each of the four parts of the question stated above. Brief comments and suggested supplemental questions follow.

Vision Creation

A critical dimension of the purpose of a board of directors is to provide effective leadership with respect to the creation of a strategic and shared vision. A *vision* is best understood as a compelling image or statement of where the leaders of an organization intend to take it and how they plan to get it there (Land and Jarman 1992, 176–182).

Practical and relatively easy to understand guidelines for assessing a board's performance regarding the 'vision thing' are suggested by the issue questions and statements in Exhibit 7.1

Exhibit 7.1

♦   Does the board regularly (e.g., annually in reviewing the CSE's plans for a fiscal year) discuss its vision of the NPS organization's future?

♦   List some particular actions the board has taken or refused to take with specific reference to creation and/or communication of a vision of what it intends for the NPS organization to be and where it plans to take the organization in the future.

♦   What evidence, if any, can be displayed to indicate how major stakeholders view the board's concept of organization purpose and vision?

♦   Does the board use its vision of the NPS organization's future as a driving force in the board's resource mobilization efforts?

♦   Describe the steps, if any, that the board has taken to see that its vision of the NPS organization's future is "shared," that is, "a vision that many people are committed to, because it reflects their own personal vision" (Senge 1990, 206).

It is the officers of the board who are particularly responsible for ensuring that the board measures and appraises its own performance. In this connection, the chairperson of the board is not simply primus inter pares. He or she bears a special burden with respect to providing leadership in overseeing the effectiveness and legitimacy of the governing board of an NPS organization.

The process of board self-appraisal involves gathering and analyzing objectively relevant information about what is happening and what should be happening. Creative use of the issue questions and statements presented in Exhibit 7.1 can make this process less difficult than it might otherwise be.

Legitimating the Organization

Chapter 1 stated and elaborated upon a crucial proposition that undergirds our model of governance of the NPS organization. The proposition affirms that in order for any NPS organization to survive, develop and remain healthy, it must have legitimacy, as an institution of the local polity in which it operates.

Therefore, a second aspect of board purpose is legitimizing (and sustaining the legitimacy of) the NPS organization in the local polity in which it exists. In my consulting practice with governing boards, I have discovered that underlying their activities is a set of preferences and controlling assumptions. They constitute the preoccupations of the board.

Evaluation of the overall performance of the board of the NPS organization should include identifying these preoccupations and assessing their impact on how well the board performs the *legitimizing* aspect of board purpose.

Several ways of going about this task are possible. One practical and useful approach is to assemble and analyze comprehensible data that will enable one to develop reasonable answers to the questions presented in Exhibit 7.2.

Exhibit 7.2

♦ How does the board explain the organization's public-interest commitments and choices of ERs to the various publics that comprise the local polity?

♦ What lines of communication, if any, has the board set up with the leadership of the major public interest groups in the local polity?

♦ How does the board justify to political leaders the requests for governmental support?

♦ Does the board have a 'sunset review' process under which every program of the NPS organization must be 're-justified' periodically?

♦ What actions has the board taken to ensure that the formats and contents of reports to external stakeholders are meaningful, from the standpoint of public accountability?

♦ How often, if at all, do officers of the board have in-depth discussions with editors and other media representatives of the organization's programs and operations?

The crucial nature of a continuing commitment to organizational legitimacy dictates that this second aspect of board self-assessment must be internally motivated. If some external entity pushes for this phase of board self-appraisal, the positive elements of its results are likely to be lessened. Individual board members may resent the time and effort involved. In summary, the leadership of the governing board's self-evaluation needs to come from the boardroom.

Obtaining Needed Resources

In other chapters of the book the author has stated unequivocally his belief that the governing board of an NPS organization has (a) the legal duty, (b) the moral obligation and (c) the authority to decide what the organization's public-interest commitments and its choices of ERs shall be.

I have also clearly expressed another strong conviction: That board members behave irresponsibly if they make these decisions and then are unwilling or refuse to take effective actions to mobilize the resources needed for effective performance of the organization. Board directors who are predisposed to behave in this manner should resign or be replaced.

Thus, the third aspect of board purpose is ensuring the availability of necessary organization resources. Any evaluation of overall performance of an NPS organization is seriously deficient if it fails to include an appraisal of the board's responsibleness with respect to resource mobilization—or more broadly development, of which resource mobilization is an integral component. In this respect, board performance measures may include a wide array of activities. Here we suggest that the questions in Exhibit 7.3 capture the essence of the most relevant criteria for such appraisal.

Exhibit 7.3

♦ Does the governing board have a systematic process for determining resource needs of the NPS organization?

♦ What type of resource mobilization strategy (see Chapter 5) does the board pursue?

♦ Does the board require or expect every board member to make an annual cash contribution to the NPS organization? (See Chapter 5.)

♦ Are there members of the board who have been recruited specifically to provide leadership of the organization's resource mobilization efforts?

♦ Does the board insist that the chief staff executive (CSE) link budget allocations to prior program decisions?

♦ How does the board communicate resource needs of the NPS organization to major stakeholder groups? Can the board articulate a clear connection between cause and effect? For example, is the board able to explain how an infusion of new resources will lead to specific outputs and eventual ERs?

♦ Does the board work with the CSE collaboratively to seek multi-year funding commitments from any of the NPS organization's funding sources?

♦ Does the board ensure that the NPS organization has an endowment program? A planned giving program?

♦ How do the CSE and the governing board coordinate pricing decisions (service charges and user fees) with other resource mobilization approaches?

Development and resource mobilization ('fund-raising' or by whatever name used) are both an art and a science. There appear to be many misconceptions about what this function is, how it should be performed, and who is responsible for it. Misconceptions aside, Chapter 5 of this book clearly stated that our model of NPS organization governance makes boards of directors ultimately responsible for resourcing the organization.

Exhibit 7.3 provides some non-technical questions, in ordinary language, which contemplates the use of informal everyday reasoning. Objective responses to these questions should generate practical indicators of the board's performance with respect to the development and the mobilization of resources for an NPS organization.

Monitoring Impact of Organization Outputs

You will recall that we have said several times throughout this book that an NPS organization is expected to offer products and services to its clients and customers—that is, outputs. But not just any kinds of outputs! The organization is expected to offer a certain type of outputs; namely, those that will fulfill the organization's public-interest commitments.

Hence the fourth and final aspect of governing board purpose shown in Figure 7.1. That aspect of our board assessment model is output monitoring,

The crucial assumption here is that the board of directors has performed its trusteeship roles (Chapter 1). And also the board's enabling and equipping roles (Chapter 5). For in performing these roles the board has been proactively involved (a) in setting public-interest commitments and (b) in determining resource requirements for the fulfillment of those commitments.

As shown in Figure 7.1, our board assessment model requires evaluation of the board's performance with respect to its activities of (1) resource mobilization and (2) monitoring the connection between quantity and quality of outputs and public-interest commitments. Performance indicators for such evaluation are suggested by the questions included in Exhibit 7.4.

Exhibit 7.4

♦   How does the board of directors satisfy itself that resource utilization is focused on the provision of outputs that further realization of the organization's public-interest commitments? Does the board require the CSE to continuously address this issue in that staff executive's reports to the board? Is this issue addressed in the organization's annual report to major stakeholders?

♦   Does the board set standards for the organization's products and services? If so, by what means does the board ensure that the standards are regularly met?

♦   What procedures does the board use to get feedback from clients, customers and other stakeholders about the quality of the organization's outputs?

♦   Does the board regularly link output considerations to all of its resource mobilization and allocation decisions?

♦   What systems and processes has the board mandated to ensure that product and service improvement and innovation will always be highly valued at the NPS organization?

In summary, the point emphasized in the discussion thus far is that evaluation of overall performance of the NPS organization starts with assessment of how well board members, as a body, do their job. In terms of substance (as contrasted with process), board assessment must:

1.   Determine whether directors continually paint a picture of the organization's future and outline a general direction toward it;

2.   Find out how well directors safeguard the legitimacy of the organization;

3.   Judge the effectiveness of directors with respect to resourcing the organization; and

4.   Appraise how well directors monitor the nexus between the organization's outputs and its public-interest commitments.

Individual Board Member Assessment

Just as the board of directors of the NPS organization, as a whole, should be evaluated for its effectiveness, so too should the board's individual members. Is the board only as good as the sum of its individual members? In fact, the sum of the board should be greater than the effectiveness of its individual members. The reason: It should reap the benefits of synergy (the $2 + 2 = 5$ concept).

The invitation to join the board of directors did not carry (or should not have carried) an implication either of a lifetime commitment or a lifetime spot. Directors are probably on a rotating cycle. That means some come up for reelection every one to three to five years. Such a process gives the board nominations committee and the chief staff executive (CSE) a chance to review the performance of individual members and to recommend changes when warranted. However, getting an individual to resign voluntarily or to refuse to run for reelection can be a very touchy issue. Experience shows that both CSEs and nomination committees face this problem with as much reluctance as the board does, when it is evident that the time has come for the CSE to step aside.

So a fair question to ask is: What makes an effective board member? At one place or another, in most of the chapters of this book, we have quoted Robert K. Mueller. He is an internationally recognized authority on boards of directors. Over two decades ago, Mueller (1978) offered a guide for evaluating the "boardworthiness" of individual board members. Here we have made only a few changes in his criteria to adapt them to the context of the NPS organization. The principle attributes Mueller looks for and the main ones he evaluates are presented below in Box 7.1.

Box 7.1 Attributes of "Boardworthiness"

Competence as Director—Experienced, trained, influential, and well respected.

Ethics—Exemplary code of behavior, morals, and values.

Ambassadorship—An enthusiastic, effective spokesperson for the organization served.

Independence—Thinks, speaks, acts independently with confidence and courage.

Preparation—Briefs self well, sincerely interested, stays up to date with the undertakings (i.e., businesses) in which the organization is engaged, and with relevant legislative and regulatory matters.

Director Practices—Asks probing questions, avoids attempting direct management of operations; acts as key resource and counsel to the executive management team and the rest of the board.

Committee Service—Usefully serves on at least one committee and does it with enthusiasm and ideas; does homework.

Organization Development—Helps win external support for the organization; seeks new clients and customers; exerts a positive force on future thinking of the organization.

Attendance—Attends all meetings, plans ahead for them, maximizes exposure to other board members, and comes well prepared to discuss issues on the agenda.

The fact that the governing board of an NPS organization is a component of a non-commercially run enterprise, rather than a commercially operated one, does not mean that Mueller's nine criteria cannot be used to design a relevant instrument for evaluating the *boardworthiness* of individual board members. In my view, the board has an obligation to establish some systematic method or procedures for periodically assessing the performance of individual directors. Such assessment involves comparison of actual performance with prior established individual-director appraisal standards.

In his consulting practice, the author has worked with some NPS organizations that have formal review periods. Typically, a review period comes at the end of each fiscal year, at which time board members evaluate one another's performance. In practice, the board chairperson or the nominations committee usually determines the evaluation process, which is relatively informal. In most of the instances that I have observed, the process focuses on (1) understanding the mission of the organization, (2) regularity of attendance at board meetings, (3) preparation for board meetings, and (4) familiarity with and understanding of financial statements and other reports.

Options may include informal discussions with each board member or anonymous written statements. Whatever the process, the objective is the same: to identify ineffective directors. If the process reveals that a board member consistently receives an evaluation of unsatisfactory from fellow directors, some action is taken. For instance, I have facilitated chairpersons' counseling board members to resign by suggesting that they are over-committed or appear to have lost interest in the organization.

Today, resignation is necessary when [board members] feel they are no longer in sinc with the philosophy or direction of the organization. If they find that to be the case, and find that their reasonable efforts to contribute to changes are rebuffed, they should resign (Mattar, 1985, 32).

If the nominations committee is not used, there appears to be great value in assigning several board members the task of planning the evaluation process and making recommendations on procedures and techniques to the full board. The board should approve the assessment tools and techniques to be employed and agree on how they will be implemented. Here we should add, parenthetically, that this entire function comes within the parameters of *controlling decisions* of the governing board. (See Chapter 2.)

The effectiveness of directors, both individually and as a board, is crucial to the overall performance of an NPS organization. That effectiveness should be assessed regularly and systematically. The assessment may be carried out through a self-appraisal process or some outside group may conduct it. In any event, to get this assessment accomplished is part of the evaluation role of the board of directors. Without this assessment, it is not likely that an NPS organization's board will come up with a credible evaluation of the overall performance of the organization.

Assessing Executive Performance

In Chapter 2 of this book we elaborated upon the proposition that in the NPS organization there is a domain of executive management. The chief staff executive (CSE) and her or his senior managers constitute an executive management team. The CSE is the leader of this team. She or he is directly accountable to the organization's governing board. Thus evaluation roles and responsibilities of the board include assessing the performance of executive management.

Boards of directors of NPS organizations are generally well aware of their responsibility for hiring the organization's CSE. Also, they are aware that they have the sole authority to fire her or him. However, somewhere between this hiring and firing authority comes responsibility for evaluating the CSE's performance. This is a responsibility boards all too often overlook or avoid.

Because of the five defining attributes of the NPS organization, assessing effectiveness and responsibleness of the executive management of any given NPS enterprise is not a simple matter. But the unavoidable difficulty can be greatly moderated if the governing behaviors of the board closely approximate the norms and standards set forth in Chapters 1, 2 and 5 of this book. The essence of the governing principles avowed in those chapters focus on (a) recognizing and intentionally fulfilling trusteeship duties, (b) carefully designing the scope of authority and responsibility of the CSE and (c) ensuring that an NPS organization is adequately equipped to accomplish board mandated public-interest commitments. The general guidelines for board action, which those chapters set forth, are listed in Exhibit 7.5.

Exhibit 7.5

♦ The board is expected to state explicitly and unequivocally the public-interest commitments of the NPS organization (Chapter 1).

♦ The board must clearly define the scope of authority or zone of discretion that the board delegates to the CSE (Chapter 2).

♦ The board is expected to state unambiguously who the first-level stakeholders of the organization are (Chapter 1).

- The board must express in specific terms the End Results (ERs) that it intends for the organization to accomplish for the benefit of its first-level stakeholders or on their behalf Chapters 1 and 5).

- It is imperative that the board outlines with reasonable specificity the ongoing reporting requirements that it expects the CSE to meet (Chapter 2).

- The board must spell out a controlling code of ethics for all organization participants.

Board adherence to these guidelines in conducting its affairs will automatically establish the essential elements of a framework for assessing executive performance. The first positive consequence is an explicit declaration of the primary societal values an NPS organization is committed to realize for its first-level stakeholders.

For example, these values may be (a) meaningful job-related training and realistic opportunities for permanent employment after training; or (b) feasible options for affordable housing for households with low incomes; or (c) safe and economical day care services for working parents with low incomes; or (d) counseling services for women who are victims of domestic violence or (e) compensatory educational experiences for targeted children.

When the board of directors clearly states the societal values such as these—i.e. public-interest commitments of an NPS organization—that must be realized for the organization's primary stakeholders, then the board can say to the CSE:

"We are going to assess your decisions and actions in terms of their impact on the realization of the stated societal values to which this organization is expressly committed."

Thus a measure of executive effectiveness is the extent to which behaviors of the CSE caused things to happen that furthered the realization of intended societal values for stakeholders. The CSE may generate many activities within the organization and between the organization and its external environment. However, if these activities fail to produce a satisfactory or acceptable amount of positive social benefits for first-level stakeholders, then the performance of the CSE may be evaluated as ineffective. This is especially the case where the board has performed well its role of resourcing the NPS organization (Chapter 5), and establishing priorities after full consultation with the CSE (Chapter 2).

It would be wonderful if the position taken in this book concerning executive effectiveness-assessment were universally accepted. But that is not the case. Many board members and a significant group of organization theorists argue that priority considerations should be given to process per se. They view as critical such process factors as 'decision making style,' 'participative management,' 'collegiality,' and an 'open door' policy. According to this view, executive effectiveness is a function of the degree of *positive-process characteristics* associated with the overall behavior of the CSE. **Of secondary importance is what happens in terms of actual value-creation for the organization's clients, customers, donors and SEinvestors.**

We do not discount these and other process considerations in assessing overall executive performance. Indeed, they are very important. Nevertheless, to give them predominant weight in an evaluation of CSE performance effectiveness is to minimize the fundamental organizational purpose that justifies the existence of an NPS organization.

Every NPS organization has a bottom line. It consists of "conditions," "states of affairs," and/or "patterns of relationships" (Kirk 1986, 50) in society to which the organization is committed, and which have value for the organization's primary stakeholders. The board needs to assess effectiveness of the CSE, as well as the organization as a whole, in terms of this bottom line, while at the same time remaining alert to process issues.

A review of Chapter 1 should remove any doubt about the author's commitment to *responsibleness* as a relevant concept in evaluating organization performance. The argument made there is that the board must establish clear standards of ethical conduct for all organization participants. This means that some methods or ways of creating value for stakeholders are deemed unacceptable on ethical grounds. Having set these standards, the board has the duty to assess CSE adherence to them. It must ensure that the general principles of "corporate social responsibility" govern executive performance.

Because of massive, largely unexamined assumptions about the inherent goodness of the 'nonprofit sector,' insufficient attention has been devoted to the ethical qualities of the behaviors of NPS organizations, including executive acts.

Some of the individual roles and responsibilities discussed in this book are *positional* in nature. That is, they are derived from the positions of directors vis-à-vis those of other organization participants. Others, in contrast, are legal in that they are associated with statutory mandates. Regardless of whether positional or legal in nature, the governing board's duty to evaluate, on an ongoing basis, the adequacy of executive management structure is crucial.

Almost always, the actual design of an NPS organization's executive management structure should be in the zone of discretion of the CSE (Chapter 2). But this principle does not negate the obligation of the board to evaluate the adequacy of that structure, in terms of its impact on realization by the organization of desired societal values. Whenever an evaluation uncovers significant weaknesses, the board must require the CSE to take appropriate corrective action.

Governing board members have no greater responsibility than that of evaluating operating management. Since the quality of executive and senior management is so critical, performance of this role in an effective manner is a key indicator of board members' contributions to the ultimate success of the NPS organization.

Some board members may be highly successful executive managers in their own right. They know that all senior-level managers in any public-serving organization have challenging, complex tasks. Therefore, they may be more inclined than other board members with different backgrounds to support NPS executive managers and understand their situations. In spite of this, all board members should be committed to ensuring that the NPS organization is managed effectively and responsibly—that it realizes sufficient societal values to justify continued support of its existence. No other body has the position, authority and duty to do this.

There is complete and absolute agreement among the twenty-six organizations [in the "sustaining Innovation" project] on the starting point for the journey to greater innovativeness: ask hard questions and [give] honest answers about why the organization exists, whom it serves, and how it will know if it is succeeding (Paul C. Light, 1998, 60).

Overall Organization Performance

Certainly assessing the effectiveness of the board of directors is very important. So also are appraising behaviors of individual board members and judging the decisions and actions of the CSE. However, in the context of the objectives of this chapter, these tasks are not regarded as ends in themselves. Each is treated as an integral part of the larger process of evaluation of the overall performance of an NPS organization.

The primary goal of this larger process is to find out how well the organization as a whole has performed during a specified period of time. At a minimum, that time frame is the prior year. Ultimately, evaluation seeks to determine the extent to which an organization is accomplishing its public-interest commitments, and, at the same time, how responsible and efficient it has been. I contend that NPS organizations and their boards must view assessment of outcomes/ERs as necessary and integral to the accomplishment of chosen public-interest commitments.

In Chapter 5, as you will recall, we urged boards to clearly state their organization's public-interest commitments. We are talking about the societal conditions, the states of affairs, and the patterns of relationships that the board has committed the organization 'to make come to pass.' According to this book's concept of NPS organization governance, these commitments are realized through the production of specific and intentionally chosen ERs.

Thus, ERs targets for the prior year are the specific impacts the board set for the organization. Overall evaluation therefore is determining how well the organization performed the prior year, in terms of reaching these ERs targets for that year. In other words, how many or what percent of the targets did the organization actually hit?

Although not simple or easy, to be sure, evaluation of overall organization performance is much less complicated or difficult than boards of directors usually think it is. In my experience, the most difficult aspect of the whole process is to get boards committed to it as a normal part of good and responsible governance. If awareness of the critical importance of performance evaluation is deeply embedded in the culture of an NPS organization, the board will not encounter difficulty in ensuring that such evaluation is carried out on an ongoing basis.

On the other hand, if the culture of the organization does not include regularly asking the Ed Koch question ("How well are we doing?"), the board of directors is likely to shirk its evaluation responsibilities.

An example of this latter situation existed in an organization with which I was associated for almost twenty years. Its mission was conducting and supporting international peace and development projects. The organization (which I will refer to as 'Organization Z') did not have formal programmatic relationships with any governmental agencies. Otherwise, it was an NPS organization—i.e., it had the remaining four defining attributes of the NPS organization.

The culture of Organization Z was clearly anti-performance evaluation. During the entire time I was associated with it, the governing board never viewed performance evaluation as part of its governance roles and responsibilities. No provision was ever made to determine actual outputs of Organization Z, or to assess the relationship of outputs to the public-interest values that were supposed to justify the enterprise's existence.

Late in 1990 Organization Z experienced a serious financial crisis. The board was persuaded to hold a special, one-day long-range planning seminar to address resource needs. But the board would not agree that some focus on performance evaluation should be part of the seminar discussion.

During the preparation for the seminar, I argued unsuccessfully that the future health of Organization Z depended on its having some form of periodic evaluation. I suggested that such evaluation could help the board identify aspects of existing programs where modifications might be justified. Moreover, the board needed the kind of information evaluations offer to make decisions on continuing or dropping particular programs, to allocate resources to programs, and to judge the overall effectiveness of Organization Z and its programs, in order to remain accountable to donors and SEinvestors.

No nonprofit organization is governed or managed perfectly and most have serious shortcomings in several areas. The ones that are most successful are able to get the board and staff to commit to a process for evaluating problems and developing a systematic way for making things better (Thomas Wolf, 1990).

The example of Organization Z also has a personal side. It highlights latent tensions associated with performing the monitoring and evaluation roles of board officers. I was treasurer of Organization Z at the time. I felt compelled to urge the board to find the cause of the organization's financial difficulties and to take proper corrective actions. It was clear to me that critical fiduciary duties of board members were involved. We had evidence that in excess of $7,500 in federal FICA and income taxes withheld from employees had not been remitted to the IRS. Instead, executive managers had used the funds to make vendor payments. My attempts to get accurate financial information and to prepare a complete financial report for the board were strongly resisted.

Moreover, my authority as treasurer and the board's monitoring authority were challenged. The board decided that only salary commitments to employees were to have a higher claim on available funds than liquidation of the IRS obligations. This decision was ignored. I received harsh criticism for my insistence on implementation of the board's decision. Subtle suggestions were made that staff morale could only be restored if I resigned as treasurer.

This experience brought home to me the reality that a board member who takes seriously his or her monitoring and evaluation duties may, in the words of Houle (1989, 146) occasionally be made to "feel like a skunk at a garden party." Houle adds, however, that the risk of incurring such animosity must be weighed "against the consequences of failing to act."

The central point of the present discussion is that monitoring and evaluating overall organizational performance has become very important instruments of accountability and control processes. Boards of directors and executive managers of NPS organizations have a long way to go before one can confidently say that they adequately understand the value of these governance instruments. It would be somewhat comforting, for instance, if the behavior of Organization Z, cited above, were the exception rather than being quite common. Unfortunately it is not.

Most boards of NPS organizations fail to ask any of the simple questions that would focus attention and energy on assessment of overall performance of their organization. In Exhibit 7.6 is a list of important questions that a board should ask if it is serious about carrying out its evaluation roles and responsibilities.

Exhibit 7.6

- How well defined are the NPS organization's choices of ERs for the next two years? The next five years? Is there a well-articulated vision that provides a blueprint for decisions and actions?
- How is the organization generally evaluated? Specifically, how is each program of the organization evaluated? Are evaluations based on

pre-established quantitative and qualitative output and outcome targets?

♦ Are all of the programs, projects and activities of the organization really needed? If so, by whom? How much would people suffer if your organization went out of business?

♦ Which of its programs, projects and services does the organization do best? How well do they meet actual needs of clients and customers? How can they be improved?

♦ How successful was the organization during the past year in setting specific ERs targets for the current year? Were both board directors and executive managers involved in the target-setting processes? Did the organization involve any of its external stakeholders in these processes?

♦ To what extent did the organization accomplish the prior year ERs targets? What resources, and in what amounts of each, were used?

♦ What special or unusual problems did the organization encounter working to achieve the prior year ERs targets? How did the organization deal with these problems?

♦ Were the governance and management systems and processes of the organization sufficient to deal with prior year problems in an effective manner? If not, what changes were made in these systems and processes?

♦ Has the organization set ERs targets for next year? If so, are any of these targets different in kind from current year ERs targets? If there is no difference, why is this so?

♦ With which entities (and activities) in its external environment does the organization compete? How well are its products and services regarded in relation to those of the competition?

♦ With what other public-serving organizations, if any, does the organization collaborate? Is there external political support for the programs of your organization? Is there external political opposition to them?

♦ Does the organization scan the environment for new sources of revenue and other resources? Does the organization have a membership base? If the answer is "yes," has the organization expanded that base within the past five years?

♦ What evidence exists to show that the organization pays attention to its clients, customers and other stakeholders? Does the organization support planned and programmed developmental experiences for its board and staff?

♦   What evidence is available to demonstrate that the organization takes seriously the matter of recruiting effective board members?

♦   What kind of orientation, if any, does the organization provide for new board members? Has the board been restructured within the past five years?

♦   How can the organization broaden its appeal to a wider group of clients, customers and donors and strengthen the loyalty of current stakeholders?

Obviously Exhibit 7.6 does not include all the questions that the members of any given board of directors should ask about the overall performance of the NPS organization they serve. Nor are they necessarily the most crucial ones in all situations. However, asking those questions will compel board members to think about the fundamentals involved in the fulfillment of the board's evaluation tasks.

Unless the board's evaluation roles—and the responsibilities they entail—are performed effectively, there can be no assurance that any NPS organization will do the right things, or even that it will do anything right. Without such assurance, the accountability and legitimacy of an NPS organization become problematic. In Chapter 1 we stated that ensuring the accountability and legitimacy of an NPS organization is an essential component of the board's trusteeship obligations. Boards have both a legal and a moral duty to give the public assurance that the organization is doing the right things and doing them right.

In a book on *Nonprofit Boards of Directors* edited by Herman and Van Til (1989), John P. Mascotte (1989, 152-159) wrote a very insightful chapter on "The Importance of Board Effectiveness in Not-for-Profit Organizations." He noted the critical difference between "doing things right" and "doing the right things." He argued that the governing board has a duty "to make sure that the organization is doing the right things." In that regard, he asserts, that board members "are not hard enough on themselves. There is typically an assumption that the purpose and values of the institution are somehow predetermined or are givens."

Mascotte argues that governing board members have a crucial obligation to ask "hard questions." Why is this so? The essence of his extensive thought-provoking response to his own question is presented below in Box 7.2.

Box 7.2
    Why is it important to ask the hard questions? The answer is simple—
public confidence determines public support...I think there are a number of organizations that chronically complain of the difficulty of achieving their objectives, of the difficulty of finding new people to support it (sic), of meeting budgets, and of getting effective community response to their programs. They'd do
well if they sat down and said, "How accurately do we measure our performance
as opposed to how the community perceives the delivery of that performance?"
As you could imagine, if the staff and particularly the board, is giving itself
"A+" in delivery when the community is in fact rating it "D-", there is going to
be a huge problem of perception that will begin to manifest itself in dozens of
ways—difficulty in getting new board members; a tendency on the part of the
staff to become more entrenched; certainly a tendency not to strike out and establish new agendas for the organization, but to stay inside the hardened little
shell of initial activity. Finally, and worse than anything else, there develops a
"Bunker" mentality that becomes very defensive and says we must guard against
all intrusion even if it appears that someone else is beginning to offer an alternative to what we do that is in fact more efficient, and better for the community
(Mascotte, 1989, 154).

    Governing boards do not have the discretion of foregoing evaluation of the
NPS organizations they serve. As noted at the beginning of this chapter, evaluation tasks are probably the most crucial of the seven sets of board roles and responsibilities. For the information obtained through evaluation of overall performance of the organizations provides feedback that boards need to successfully carry out the other duties discussed in previous chapters of the book.

    By being informed, through evaluation reports, about the performance of
the organizations, and about their present strengths and weaknesses, governing
boards are able to make better decisions about future directions and strategies.
A critical governance obligation of the board of any NPS organization is to define and keep analyzing and testing the reason for continued existence of the
enterprise.

    A couple of times, in previous chapters of this book, we have referred to
Peter Drucker's (1980, 1) statement about the "first task" of organization leaders
in turbulent times; namely,

to make sure of the institution's capacity for survival, to make sure of its structural strength and soundness, of its capacity to survive a blow, to adapt to sudden change, and to avail itself of new opportunities.

The central message of this chapter is that without some type of evaluation of overall performance of NPS organizations, governing boards simply cannot carry out this "first task" very well. That is to say, unless boards of directors regularly examine themselves and the organizations they serve with a self-critical eye, they cannot reliably know the strengths and weaknesses of the organizations, whether the organizations can or cannot adapt to sudden changes, or how capable they are of taking advantage of new opportunities. And without such knowledge, boards simply cannot govern effectively and responsibly. 1

---

1. The following excerpt from a recent news article is a dramatic illustration of what may happen when a board of directors fails to effectively fulfill its organizational evaluation responsibilities.

SCHOOL SYSTEM BIDS TO TAKE OVER HEAD START

The Arlington [Virginia] school system is seeking to take over the county's Head Start program for disadvantaged children after the nonprofit organization that had run it for many years was closed in June in response to revelations of significant accounting lapses.

The accounting troubles that led to closure of the nonprofit Arlington Community Action Program (ACAP) surprised some county leaders...The audit was "clearly devastating," said Arlington County Board member Barbara A. Ravola (D), who is also a member of ACAP's board. She said ACAP board members were caught off guard by the findings. "I was just flabbergasted," she said.

SOURCE: *The Washington Post*, September 14, 2006, Section B, p 5.

CODA

The growing complexity of society's work and the changing social values have led to a recognition that historical organizational forms are no longer adequate for meeting society's needs. ...Thus it appears that the distinction between "private for profit" vs. "public not-for-profit" organizations is inadequate, either for explaining behavior or for designing new socially responsive forms—H. Igor Ansoff, *Strategic Management* (1979).

Although not frequently acknowledged, there is tremendous diversity among organizations that have a *legally defined* not-for-profit (LDNFP) status. Even within the large group of organizations that are exempt from federal income taxation under Section 501(c)(3) of the U. S. Internal Revenue Code, there exists a great amount of diversity.

In the *Preface*, in the *Introduction*, and in the seven chapters of **BOARD MEMBERS:** *Governing Roles and Responsibilities*, I have hypothesized that five organizational factors may be utilized to delineate a distinct subcategory of not-for-profit organizations. The five organizational factors are:

- A self-declared, explicitly articulated public-serving mission.
- Nongovernmental ownership, governance and management.
- A multiplicity of relationships with governmental agencies and programs.
- Substantial, if not exclusive, noncommercial operations.
- Corporate entity status through formal incorporation.

In the book I employed these five organizational factors to define a discrete subcategory of not-for-profit entities. I called them NPS (nongovernmental public-serving) organizations.1

---

1. After reading the book in manuscript form, two former academic colleagues have written to inquire whether institutions of higher education may be included in my subcategory of NPS organizations. Many educational institutions share all five of the organizational attributes this book uses. Those educational institutions are NPS enterprises.

With respect to NPS organizations, the book articulated a second hypothesis: **These enterprises have to be led, guided, directed and controlled.** This cybernetic function is presumed to exist in two domains of the NPS organization—(1) a domain of governance and (2) a domain of executive level management.

The book assumed that within the domain of governance the board of directors has ultimate authority, which includes a duty to design a structure of delegated authority for the chief staff executive of the NPS organization.

In the book I articulated a seven-dimensional concept of the governing roles and responsibilities of boards. And I argued—persuasively, I hope—that the board of directors of an NPS organization has both a legal and a moral duty:

- To ensure that the organization fulfills its trusteeship obligations effectively, efficiently and responsibly.
- To monitor on an ongoing basis the performance of the chief staff executive of the organization.
- To facilitate organizational learning.
- To act as a catalyst when the legitimacy and viability of the NPS organization require catalytic board behaviors.
- To assure that the organization is adequately equipped and resourced to carry out its public-interest commitments.
- To establish and maintain inter-organizational linkages and networks.
- To evaluate organizational performance, including the performance of the board itself.

In this connection, I attempted throughout the book to explain as clearly and as meaningfully as possible another major premise: **Boards of directors of NPS organizations face enormously more difficult governing challenges than boards of other types of not-for-profit entities.**

While difficult governance challenges face all boards of NPS organization, they affect community-based ones more severely. That is partially due to the fact that they are less likely to continuously recruit and retain the quality of needed boardroom talent.

I hope the discussions presented in the book convey my cautious optimism that all NPS organization boards of directors can meet the challenges they face. A primary reason I wrote the book is to further boardroom *learning cultures* that will help boards to govern NPS organizations in the future more effectively and responsibly than they generally do presently, or than they have done in the recent past.

With respect to the achievement of that goal, two target audiences of the book can make critical contributions. They are (1) the directors and teachers of college and university courses in nonprofit organization governance/leadership and (2) board development consultants and trainers.

I encourage the participants of both of these audience-groups to acknowledge the reality that NPS organizations are empirically distinguishable from other entities that coexist in what is popularly referred to as the *nonprofit world* or the *voluntary sector*.

One need not buy into the concept of a "shadow statue apparatus" (Wolch, 1990) in order to affirm the continuation today of massive restructuring of the American welfare state. That restructuring places extra burdens on NPS organizations. But it also presents some new opportunities for NPS organizations to help in creative ways to shape societal policies that may result in greater measures of social justice for marginalized individuals and groups.

A presumption of the book is that boards of directors of NPS organizations have both the power and the duty to help determine the place of nongovernmental public-serving entities in the institutional fabric of any overall reorganized American welfare state. My ultimate hope is that the book provides some useful guidelines for NPS organizations' boards, as they steer their enterprises through the unplanned, unpredictable, and frightening to some, expansion of what Weidenbaum (1969) described as "the modern public sector." Thirty-seven years ago Weidenbaum applied this description to the then rapidly developing phenomena of

"(1) a widespread reliance upon government-oriented corporations and other quasi-private organizations that perform government functions under close surveillance; (2) a massive use of advanced research concepts and high technology; (3) shifting relationships between federal and state governments, with more funds coming from the former and more of the end activities performed by the latter; and (4) government expansion into areas for which traditional public agencies are not well equipped but in which private markets do not exist to any significant degree."

The discussions in the book have dealt extensively with ensuring and sustaining the legitimacy, integrity and viability of NPS organizations in light of the impact of the dynamics of *the modern public sector*. Absent a clear understanding of these dynamics within the boardroom of the NPS organization, that enterprise simply cannot properly and creatively influence the evolution of the broader governance of governmental institutions with which it interacts.

Typically, executive and legislative leaders of federal and state governments are neither clear nor consistent in their reasons for relying on NPS organizations to help implement governmental policies and programs. And most NPS boards of directors have not articulated a clear and consistent rationale for their willingness to enter into diverse patterns of relationships with governmental agencies.

In almost every important societal setting conceivable, the purposes of governmental agencies and those of NPS organizations may (a) coincide, (b) run parallel to each other, or (c) go in sharply divergent directions. Each of these possibilities poses dilemmas for democratic and responsible governance of both NPS organizations and executive and legislative bodies of federal and state governments.

In the book's *Preface*, I stated the following viewpoint: "Society needs reasoned decisions concerning the appropriateness of present institutional arrangements involving NPS organizations. It also needs sound judgments regarding issues of whether these arrangements properly reflect essential governing board functions."

I will end this Coda statement by simply sharing my vision with those of you who have read, or plan to examine, the text material.

My vision is that the book will stimulate the kinds of serious inquiries and focused discussions—by boards of directors, by governmental leaders, by foundation executives, by consultants, and by organization theory professors at colleges and universities—that may illuminate the dilemmas alluded to above.

I believe such inquiries and discussions are needed now, more than ever before, to help keep our core institutions viable, vibrant, democratic, and morally responsible.

Today the community-based NPS enterprise is more than just another 'nonprofit organization.' It is a key institutional component of the American political economy. It has a purpose that encompasses facilitating the achievement of a greater measure of *social justice* "for the least of those among us." The men and women who occupy its boardroom have a legal and moral duty to ensure that the NPS organization fulfills this purpose—effectively, efficiently and responsibly.

Appendix 1
List of Abbreviations

CAA	=	Community action agency
CAN	=	Center for Nonprofit Advancement
CSE	=	Chief staff executive
EOA	=	Economic Opportunity Act of 1964, as amended
ER	=	End results
IR	=	Instrumental results
LDNFP	=	Legally defined not-for-profit
MANO	=	Maryland Association of Nonprofit Organizations
NPS	=	Nongovernmental public-serving
Triple L	=	Life-long-learning
ULOC	=	Unrecognized latent organizational crisis
WIA	=	Workforce Investment Act

GLOSSARY

End Results: These are the actual *societal outcomes* of the output of goods and services that an NPS organization produces.

Governance: Term denotes decisions and actions of boards of directors of NPS organizations aimed at leading, guiding, directing, and controlling them, including the performance of their executive management.

Instrumental Results: This term refers to effects of the activities and operations of an NPS organization that produce or lead to End Results.

Legally defined not-for-profit status: The phrase refers to a status that some competent governmental jurisdiction has granted an organization, including certain associated prescriptions, proscriptions, powers, and privileges.

Nongovernmental organization: An organization that is not owned, or directly governed, or directly managed by some governmental entity.

Public-interest commitments: Term refers to the positive social impacts that an NPS organization intends to produce through its activities and operations.

Public-serving: The act of offering an NPS organization's goods and services to the general public, or broadly defined segments of the general public, rather than only to the organization's members, supporters and directors.

"SEinvestment:" This term refers to investing in the mission of an NPS organization by a person or group motivated by a desire to receive both *financial returns* and *social-outcome returns* from the resources provided.

Appendix 2

Book's Theoretical Foundation

> The function of theory…is not simply to provide "explanations"; it is also to raise useful questions and, perhaps most important, to identify the most fruitful unit of analysis for coming to grips with the central problem in a field—Salamon (1995, 18).

As I understand the term 'theory,' it refers to a set of systematically related statements, including an empirically testable generalization. The concepts that comprise the language of the theory must have *observable* referents. That is, they must be such that their existence can be verified by examining the phenomena.

Undergirding all of the principal arguments of each chapter of this book are six theoretical propositions and three inferences drawn from the propositional statements. The following are the propositional statements.

1. Some organizations have a primary *public* purpose. They are established to serve interests and needs of society as a whole, or some broadly defined segment of society. (The book refers to them as *public-serving* organizations.)

2. Some organizations have a primary *nonpublic* purpose. They are established to serve interests and needs of their members, supporters, founders or sponsors. (The book calls them *nonpublic-serving* organizations.)

3. Some public-serving organizations are *nongovernmental* entities. They are not part of the formal structures of any governmental institutions. In contrast, other public-serving organizations are *governmental* entities. Each is formally included in some governmental structure.

4. Some public-serving organizations are operated on a *non-commercial* basis. Their operating costs are not entirely covered from

earned revenues. In contrast, other public-serving organizations are operated *commercially*. They obtain sufficient amounts of earned revenues from economic transactions in the marketplace to defray operating costs (including the cost of capital).

5. The more formalized and complex public-serving organizations are *incorporated*. They are corporations. Some have a *legally defined not-for-profit (LDNFP) status*. Consequently, their governance and management have to conform to the prescriptions and proscriptions of the LDNFP status.

6. Both governmental and nongovernmental public-serving organizations may have the LDNFP status. Similarly, both noncommercially operated and commercially run public-serving organizations may be granted such status.

From these six theoretical propositions, I have drawn the following inferences, some of which may include elements of value judgments.

1. Based on the propositions stated above, one may logically assume a *class of organizations* that (a) are nongovernmental, (b) have public-serving purposes, (c) are operated noncommercially, (d) have many formal relationships with governmental institutions, and (e) possess the LDNFP status. (In the book, for the sake of brevity and convenience, I call this class of entities *nongovernmental public-serving [NPS] organizations*.)

2. Because of special relationships with governmental institutions, NPS organizations have substantial dimensions of *"publicness."*

3. In view of the fact that this class of organizations has substantial dimensions of publicness, boards of directors of the organizations must be viewed as critical functioning parts of the enterprises' cybernetic systems and processes.

Figure A-1 below presents a schematic model of the organization classification concept that the propositional statements and associated inferences involve.

Figure A-1. An Organization Classification Model

*Public*Serving		*Non*Public-Serving
N **O** **N** **G** **O** **V**	*NonGov-PS* **A**	**B** *NonGov-NonPS*
	C	**D**
G **O** **V**	*Gov-PS*	*Gov-NonPS*

LEGEND:

Gov	=	Governmental
NonGov	=	*Non*Governmental
NonPS	=	*Non*public-Serving
PS	=	Public-Serving

In Figure A-1 above, all organizations in Quadrants **A** and **B** are *nongovernmental*, and all those in Quadrants C and D are *governmental*.

Quadrants **A** and **C** include *public-serving* organizations, and Quadrants **B** and **D** include *nonpublic-serving* organizations.

Any organization in either Quadrant A or Quadrant C may be granted a legally defined not-for-profit (LDNFP) status.

The governing boards that are the subject of this book are all part of the cybernetic systems and processes of organizations included in Quadrant A.

Generally speaking, academics and commentators do not define their categories of "nonprofit organizations." They usually accept the categories the IRS recognizes as exempt from federal taxation under Section 501(c) of the United States Internal Revenue Code. Most often, academics and commentators limit their discussion to organizations recognized as tax exempt pursuant to Section 501 (c)(3), the ones tax attorneys call "public charities."

It should be noted here that not all of the entities exempt from federal income taxation can qualify for inclusion in our subcategory of NPS organizations. That is because some tax-exempt organizations are not operated *noncommercially*. Others do not normally have relationships with governments, which means that they are not used by governmental agencies to deliver products and services to the public or broadly defined segments of the public. Finally, some tax-exempt organizations do not meet our requirement of an explicitly stated "public-serving" mission.

Appendix 3
Board Management

Nonprofit boards are the first and last line of defense against poor performance, corruption, and lack of accountability. They are supposed to be the protectors of the public interest. The buck stops with them. That, at least, is the theory. In practice, it often doesn't work that way (Pablo Eisenberg, 2002).

Board Management Process

The discussions in the Introduction and seven chapters of this book should clearly establish the fact that I do not share an opinion frequently expressed in much of the conventional literature. It is the viewpoint that boards of directors of enterprises, like the NPS organization, have "an unclear legal status" (Middleton, 1987, 142). It may be accurate to say that "What the full responsibility of being a [director]...means is often ambiguous" (Mueller, 1990, 103). However, the legal authority associated with this responsibility is generally not ambiguous, at least not to me. Regardless of variations in the language of particular statutes, the law authorizes governing boards to:

- Define and redefine, when necessary, the mission concept, public-interest commitments, and major policies of the organization.
- Ensure the effectiveness and responsibleness of the organization as a whole through the board's oversight of staff and other activities.
- Sustain the image and legitimacy of the organization among its stakeholders through reports, visits, talks, hearing of grievances, issuance of statements, etc.

- Provide for the financial stability of the organization by securing necessary resources and monitoring management of the budgetary process.
- Select, hold accountable and remove the chief staff executive.
- Sustain the continuity of the board, generally by utilizing the structured device of a nominating committee.

In my experience, the critical problem has not been, and is not now, unclear legal authority and status of the board of directors—at least in those organizations with articles of incorporation and operating bylaws that provide for a governing board of directors. Rather, it has been, and continues to be, how to ensure the accountability of the board itself, particularly where the board is self-perpetuating. The key question is:

What can be done, and by whom, in those all too often situations where it is clearly obvious that the board has not fulfilled its trusteeship duty by a failure to exercise its legal authority, or where the authority has been exercised in arbitrary and irresponsible ways?

I believe that one way to begin addressing this critical issue is for every governing board of NPS organizations to establish and maintain a formal board management process. Below in this Appendix are some components and elements that should be incorporated in such a board management process.

Standards of Responsible Board Processes

1.   A board of directors of the NPS organization should schedule at least four regular meetings each year to coincide with the organization's need for decisions regarding matters that are properly the responsibility of the board.

2.   The board chairperson and the chief staff executive (CSE) should jointly develop an agenda for each meeting, together with supporting materials. The agenda, along with the supporting materials, should be sent to each board member at least ten days in advance of the scheduled meeting date. The circulation of such material in advance of the meeting will provide the members with time to consider the matters to be acted on at the meeting. This practice should make discussion of agenda items more meaningful.

3.   The board should have an executive committee empowered to act on its behalf between regularly scheduled meetings to deal with matters requiring the action of directors and which cannot wait until the next regular board meeting. Care, however, should be taken to ensure that the executive committee does not become a vehicle for circumventing full board consideration of matters that can and should wait for action until the next regular meeting. In this regard, it is prudent practice to have the full board ratify all actions taken by the executive committee.

4.   The board should establish a reasonable number of standing committees that are related to broad policy areas of the organization. There should at least be a planning and resource allocations committee; a management or operations committee; an evaluations committee; and a nominations committee. Unlike the executive committee, normally standing committees should not be authorized to act on behalf of the full board. Generally, standing committees should be responsible for keeping the board informed regarding matters that fall within the scope of their job description.

5.   After each meeting of the board, and of any of its standing committees, minutes thereof should be prepared promptly. These minutes should be circulated to all members of the board and be accepted at the next meeting of the board of directors. The one exception to this practice is that minutes of standing committees may not need to be circulated if the committees' meetings immediately precede a full board meeting at which activities of such committees are reported and included in the regular board meeting minutes.

6.   The CSE should be an ex officio nonvoting member of the board of directors. He or she should attend all meetings of the board (except when the board is formally evaluating the executive's performance) and of its executive committee and should also have a right to attend any meeting of the board's standing committees. As the chief executive manager selected by the board to manage the organization governed by the board, this top staff person will present recommendations for action on which he or she has already taken a position. Therefore he or she should not vote on his or her own recommendations, but should have the right to discuss with the board the reasons for them, and to hear the board's discussions regarding their acceptability or unacceptability. In addition, the board should rely on the CSE to present to it the current status of operations, problems, and opportunities from his or her staff perspective.

7. The board should seriously regard itself as answerable to the organization's major publics or primary stakeholders. It is accountable for establishing the policies under which the organization must operate. While it must monitor the effectiveness and efficiency of organizational operations, the board should avoid interference in clearly managerial matters. Its monitoring activities should result primarily from reviewing the various reports of the CSE covering the operations of the organization. The board should ensure that these reports come to it on a regular basis.

8. The board, or at a minimum the management or operations committee, should meet independently with the appointed external audit firm to review the results of the annual audit of the organization's operations as well as the findings included in the audit firm's management letter. Particularly attention should be paid to any findings of deficiencies in fiscal management or internal controls.

9. The full board or the executive committee should conduct a formal evaluation of the performance of the CSE on a regular basis, consistent with the terms of this executive's appointment. The board and the CSE should mutually agree in advance to these terms.

10. The board should regularly conduct a systematic assessment of its organization and performance. Through this assessment the board can determine whether the organization structure and/or membership characteristics of the board need to be changed.

11. The board should make provisions for carefully planned orientation experiences for all new board members. These experiences should be designed to emphasize the critical responsibilities of directorships and the unique characteristics of the NPS organization. Active participation in these experiences should be required of all new board members.

12. In today's changing environment of directorate roles and responsibilities, the operations of the board of directors of the NPS organization should be conducted in accordance with a set of published Bylaws. These Bylaws should be consistent with any limitations that are set forth in the organization's charter or articles of incorporation. At a minimum, the Bylaws should cover:

- The responsibilities and powers of the board, and major functions such as:
  - Selection of the chief executive manager;
  - Selection of directors to fill vacancies;
  - Selection of external auditors and legal counsel;

> ➤ Determination and systematic review of the organization' mission concept and public-interest commitments.

♦ Board membership, including the number of members authorized, terms of office, number of classes, and mandatory retirement (if any);

♦ The officers of the board and such officers of the organization as are deemed appropriate, including the terms and duties of each officer;

♦ The time and place of regularly scheduled meetings of the board, including the identification of the meeting that is considered the annual meeting of the board;

♦ The committees of the board, their composition and responsibilities;

♦ The indemnification of members, officers, and managers; and

♦ The process required for amending the Bylaws.

In 1982, an association of community action agencies (CAAs) asked me to develop for its member CAAs a monograph describing the characteristics of an effective board of directors. The monograph I presented to the association included the following summary description of what I viewed as essential attributes of an effective directorate twenty-four years ago. They are still relevant.

ESSENTIAL CHARACTERISTICS OF AN EFFECTIVE BOARD OF DIRECTORS

Diversity—The board as a whole contains differences in talents, skills, experiences, interests, and social backgrounds.

Structure—The board is organized in such a way that individuals and committees assume proper and active roles in its functioning.

Member Involvement—Directors demonstrate a high degree of interest in their roles and responsibilities. They are genuinely concerned about the enterprise's operations and the social forces that affect production and delivery of goods and services by the enterprise.

Knowledge—Directors are well-informed regarding problems, present capabilities, and future prospects of the enterprise.

Rapport—Directors have mutual respect for each other regardless of differences of opinion, and maintain a productive working relationship with each other.

Sensitivity—The board is representative of, and sensitive to, different constituencies and viewpoints.

Sense of Priorities—Directors are concerned with important and long-term issues, not matters of a trivial nature.

Direction—The chairperson is respected, and is strong and skilled in making certain that various points of view are expressed in reaching satisfactory decisions.

Strength—The board is strong enough to achieve effective policy decisions. Importunities of special interests or the bureaucratic interests of governmental agencies do not overpower it.

Financial Support—The board contains a reasonable number of directors who can be effective in obtaining financial support for the enterprise.

Board-CEO Relationships—There is a productive working relationship between the chief executive officer and directors.

Accomplishments—The board has a genuine sense of progress and achievement, and directors generally gain satisfaction from their board service.

References

Allison, Graham T. (1971). *Essence of Decision.* Boston: Little,
    Brown and Company.
Ansoff, H. Igor (1979). *Strategic Management.* New York: John
    Wiley &Sons.
_____(1973). "Management in Transition." In Edward C. Bursk
    (Edited), *Challenge to Leadership.* New York: The Free Press.
Anthony, Robert N. (1988). *The Management Control Function.*
    Cambridge: Harvard University Press.
Anthony, Robert N and Regina E. Herzlinger (1980, Revised Edition).
    Management Control in Nonprofit Organizations. Homewood,
    IL:Richard D. Irwin, Inc.
Banovetz, James (1971) (Editor). *Managing the Modern City.*
    Washington, DC: International City Management
    Association.
Barnard, Chester I. (1938). *The Functions of the Executive.*
    Cambridge: Harvard University Press.
Bartunek, J. M. (1984). "Changing Interpretive Schemes and
    Organizational Restructuring: The Example of a Religious
    Order." *Administrative Science Quarterly,* 29:355-372.
Bellah, Robert N. (1985). *Habits of the Heart.* New York: Basic Books.
Ben-Ner, Avner and Theresa Van Hoomissen (1993). "Nonprofit
    Organizations in the Mixed Economy." In Ben-Ner, Avner and
    Benedetto Gui (Edited), *TheNon-profit Sector in the Mixed Economy*
    Ann Arbor: University of Michigan Press.
Benkler, Yochai (2006). *The Wealth of Networks: How Social Production*
    Transforms Markets and Freedom. New Haven, CT: Yale Uniersity
    Press.
Bennett, James T. and J. DiLorenzo (1989). *Unfair Competition: The*
    Profits of Nonprofits. Lanham, MD: Hamilton Press.
Bennis, Warren and Burt Nanus (1985). *Leaders.* New York: Harper
    and Row.
Berger, Peter L. and Richard J. Neuhaus (1977). *To Empower People.*
    Washington, DC: American Enterprise Institute.

Blanchard, Kenneth and Norman V. Peale (1988). *The Power of Ethical Management.* New York: William Morrow and Company.

Borst, Diane and Patrick J. Montana (1977). *Managing Nonprofit Organizations.* New York: AMACOM.

Boulding, Kenneth E. (1973). "Intersects: The Peculiar Organizations." In Edward Bursk (Edited), *Challenge to Leadership.* New York: The Free Press.

_____ (1953). *The Organizational Revolution.* New York: Harper

Bower, Joseph L. (1983). *The Two Faces of Management.* Boston: Houghton Mifflin Company.

Bozeman, Barry (1987). *All Organizations Are Public.* San Francisco: Jossey-Bass Publishers.

Brunsson, Nils (1985). *The Irrational Organization.* New York: John Wiley and Sons.

Bryson, John M. (1988). *Strategic Planning for Public and Nonprofit Organizations.* San Francisco: Jossey-Bass Publishers.

Burns, James M. (1978). *Leadership.* New York: Harper & Row.

Carver, John (1990). *Boards That Make a Difference.* San Francisco: Jossey-Bass Publishers.

Chawla, Sarita and John Renesch (1995) (Editors). *Learning Organizations: Developing Cultures for Tomorrow's Workplace.* Portland, OR: Productivity Press

Cleveland, Harlan (1972). *The Future Executive.* New York: Harper and Row.

Crimmins, James C. and Mary Keil (1983). *Enterprise in the Nonprofit Sector.* Washington, DC: Partners for Liverable Places.

Crosby, Philip B. (1988). *The Eternally Successful Organization.* New York: McGraw-Hill.

Culbert, Samuel A. and John J. McDonough (1985). *Radical Management.* New York: The Free Press.

Cyert, Richard M. (1975). *The Management of Nonprofit Organizations.* Lexington, MA: D. C. Heath.

_____ and James G. March (1963). *A Behavioral Theory of The Firm.* Englewood Cliffs, NJ: Prentice-Hall.

DeGreene, Kenyon B. (1982). *The Adaptive Organization.* New York: John Wiley and Sons.

Derthick, Martha (1970). *The Influence of Federal Grants.* Cambridge: Harvard University Press.

Donahue, John D. (1989). *The Privatization Decision.* New York: Basic Books.

Douglas, James (1987). "Political Theories of Nonprofit Organizations." In Walter W. Powell (Edited), *The Nonprofit Sector.* New Haven: Yale University Press.

Dowling, John and Jeffrey Pfeffer (1975). "Organizational Legitimacy: Social Values and Organizational Behavior. " *Pacific Sociological Review*, 18, No. 1 (January).

Drucker, Peter F. (1990). *Managing the Nonprofit Organization.* New York: HarperCollings Publishers.

_____ (1989). *The New Realities.* New York: Harper & Row.

_____ (1980). *Managing in Turbulent Times.* New York: Harper & Row.

_____ (1974). *Management: Tasks, Responsibilities and Practices.* New York: Harper & Row.

_____(1968). *The Age of Discontinuity.* New York: Harper & Row.

Duca, Diane J. (1996). *Nonprofit Boards: Roles, Responsibilities and Performance.* Oryx Press

Eadie, Douglas C. (1994). *Boards That Work: A Practical Guide to Building Effective Association Boards.* Washington, DC: American Society of Association Executives.

Eisenberg, Pablo (2005). *Challenges for Nonprofits and Philanthropy.* Medford, MA: Tufts University Press.

Elazar, Daniel J. (1971). *Cities of the Prairie.* New York: Basic Books.

Emerson, Jed and Fay Twersky (1996). *Social Entrepreneurs: The Success, Challenge and Lessons of Non-Profit Enterprise Creation.* San Francisco, CA: The Roberts Foundation

Etzioni, Amitai (1996). *The New Golden Rule.* New York: Basic Books

_____(1984). *An Immodest Agenda.* New York: McGraw-Hill.

_____ (1973). "The Third Sector and Domestic Missions." *Public Administration Review* (July/August (1973).

Fink, Justin (1989). "Community Agency Boards of Directors: Viability and Vestigiality, Substance and Symbol." In Robert D. Herman and Jon Van Til (Edited), *Nonprofit Boards of Directors.* New Brunswick: Transaction Publishers.

Foy, Nancy (1980). *The Yin and Yang of Organizations.* New York: William Morrow and Company.

Freeman, R. Edward (1983). "Strategic Management: A Stakeholder's View." In Robert Lamb (Edited), *Advances in Strategic Management.* Greenwich, CT: JAI Press.

Gailbraith, J. R. and Robert K. Kazanjian (1988). "Strategy, Technology, and Emerging Organizational Forms." In Jerald Hage (Edited), *Futures of Organizations.* Lexington, MA: D.C. Heath.

Garratt, Bob (1987). *The Learning Organization.* Aldershot, England: Gower Publishing Company.

Gawthrop, Louis C. (1984). *Public Sector Management, Systems, and Ethics.* Bloomington, IN: Indiana University Press.

Gies, David L., J. Steven Ott, and Jay M. Shafritz (1990). *The Nonprofit Organization.* Belmont, CA: Brooks/Cole Publishing Company.

Gortner, Harold F., Julianne Mahler, and Jeanne B. Nicholson (1987). *Organization Theory.* Chicago: The Dorsey Press.

Gray, Barbara (1989). *Collaborating: Finding Common Ground for Multiparty Problems.* San Francisco: Jossey-Bass

Grace, Kay Sprinkel (1997). *Beyond Fund raising: New strategies for Nonprofit Innovation and Investment.* New York: John Wiley & Sons

Greenleaf, Robert K. (1977). *Servant Leadership.* New York: Paulist Press.

Greer, Scott (1972). *The Urban View.* New York: Oxford University Press.

Gross, Bertram M. (1968). *Organizations and Their Managing.* New York: The Free Press.

Gui, Benedetto (1993). "The Economic Rationale for the 'Third Sector.'" In Ben-Ner, Avner and Benedetto Gui (Edited), *The Nonprofit Sector in the Mixed Economy.* Ann Arbor: University of Michigan Press.

Hage, Jerald (1998). "Reflections on Emotional Rhetoric and Boards for Governance of NPOs." In Walter W. Powell and Elisabeth S. Clemens (Ed.), *Private Action and the Public Good.* New Haven: Yale University Press.

_____ (1988). "The Pathways of Evolution in Organizations." In Jerald Hage (Edited), *Futures of Organizations.* Lexington, MA: D. C. Heath.

_____ (1980). *Theories of Organizations.* New York: John Wiley & Sons.

Haller, Leon (1982). *Financial Resources Management for Nonprofit Organizations.* Englewood Cliffs, NJ: Prentice-Hall.

Handy, Charles (1993). *Understanding Organizations.* New York: Oxford University Press.

_____ (1990). *The Age of Unreason.* Boston: Harvard Business School Press.

Hansmann, Henry B. (1980). "The Role of Nonprofit Enterprise." *Yale Law Journal,* 89:835-901.

Harris, Philip R. (1985). *Management in Transition.* San Francisco: Jossey-Bass Publishers.

Harvey, Donald F. (1982). *Strategic Management.* Columbus, OH: Charles E. Merrill Publishing Company.

Heifetz, Ronald A. (1994). *Leadership Without Easy Answers.* Cambridge, MA: Harvard University Press.

Henn, Harry G. and John R. Alexander (1983). *Corporations* (3rd Edition). St. Paul: West Publishing Company.

Herman, Robert D. (1989). "Concluding Thoughts on Closing the Board Gap. " In Robert D. Herman and Jon Van Til (Edited), *Nonprofit Boards of Directors.* New Brunswick, NJ: Transaction Publishers.

_____ and Jon Van Til (Edited) (1989). *Nonprofit Boards of Directors.* New Brunswick,NJ: Transaction Publishers.

Hickman, Craig R. (1990). *Mind of a Manager, Soul of a Leader.* New York: John Wiley and Sons.

Hiltz, Starr Roxanne and Murray Turoff (1978). *The Network Nation.* Reading, MA: Addison-Wesley Publishing Company.

Hirschman, A. O. (1970). *Exit, Voice, and Loyalty.* Cambridge: Harvard University Press.

Hoffman, Frank & Bill Withers (1995). "Shared Values: Nutrients for Learning." In Sarita Chawla and John Renesch (Editors), *Learning Organizations: Developing Cultures for Tomorrow's Workplace.* Portland, OR: Productivity Press.

Hood, Christopher (1984). *The Hidden Public Sector.* Glasglow: University of Strathclyde.

Hosmer, LaRue T. (1987). *The Ethics of Management.* Homewood, IL: Richard D. Irwin.

Houle, Cyril O. (1989). *Governing Boards.* San Francisco: Jossey -Bass Publishers.

Jackall, Robert (1988). *Moral Mazes: The World of Corporate Managers.* New York: Oxford University Press.

Howe, Fisher (1995). *Welcome To The Board: Your Guide to Effective Participation.* San Francisco: Jossey-Bass

Janis, Irving L. (1983). *Groupthink.* Boston: Houghton Mifflin Company.

Jenkins, J. Craig (1987). "Nonprofit Organizations and Policy Advocacy." In Walter Powell (Edited), T*he Nonprofit Sector.* New Haven: Yale University Press.

Kanter, Rosabeth M. (1989). *When Giants Learn To Dance.* New York: Simon and Schuster.

_____(1983). *The Change Masters.* New York: Simon and Schuster.

Kanter, Rosabeth M. and David V. Summers (1987). "Doing Well While Doing Good: Dilemmas of Performance Measurement in Nonprofit Organizations and the Need for a Multiple -Constituency Approach." In Walter Powell (Edited), The *Nonprofit Sector.* New Haven: Yale University Press.

Kastens, Merrit L. (1980). *REdefining the Manager's Job.* New York: AMACOM.

Kast, Freemont E. and James E. Rosenzweig (1979) (3rd Edition). *Organization and Management.* New York: McGraw-Hill.

Kenny, Sean D. (1986). "Functions, Authority, and Roles of the Board of Directors." In Chapman, Harold E. et al., *The Contemporary Director.* Saskatoon, Canada: Cooperative League of Canada.

Kirk, W. Astor (1986). *Nonprofit Organization Governance: A Challenge In Turbulent Times.* New York: Carlton Press.

_____ (1985). *Socio-Economic Investing* (Processed). Suitland, MD: Policy Management Services, Inc., P. O Box 470.

_____ (1979). *Objectives-Oriented Executive Management.* Indianapolis, IN: Third Annual Executive Management Institute, National Community Action Agency Executive Directors Association.

_____ (1978). *Are the Major Perspectives on CAA Regimes Relevant?* Philadelphia: U. S. Community Services Administration.

_____ (1966). "Statement on Judicial Review. Hearings Before the Subcommittee on Constitutional Rights. " U. S. Senate (89th Cong., 2nd Sess., March 9, 1966), Washington, DC.

_____ (1958). Television Allocation Policy: An Administrative Search for the Public Interest. Ph.D. Dissertation (*Dissertation Abstracts*, Vol. XIX, No. 9).

Kline, Peter & Bernard Saunders (1998,2[nd] Edition). *Ten Steps to A Learning Organization.* Arlington, VA: Great Ocean Publishers.

Kofman, Fred & Peter Senge (1995). "Communities of Commitment: The Heart of Learning Organizations." In Sarita Chawla and John Renesch (Editors), *Learning Organizations: Developing Cultures for Tomorrow's Workplace.* Portland, OR: Productivity Press.

Kolderie, Ted (1984). "Business Opportunities in the Changing Conceptions of the Public Sector Role." In Harvey Brooks, Lance Liebman, and Corinne Schelling (Editors), *Public-Private Partnership.*Cambridge: Ballinger.

Koteen, Jack (1989). *Strategic Management in Public and Nonprofit Organizations.* New York: Praeger.

Kotler, Philip (1982). *Marketing for Nonprofit Organizations.* Englewood Cliffs, NJ: Prentice-Hall.

Kotter, J. P. (1988). *The Leadership Factor.* New York: The Free Press.

Kouzes, James M and Barry Z. Posner (1987). *The Leadership Challenge.* San Francisco: Jossey-Bass, Publishers

Kramer, R. M. (1985). "Towards a Contingency Model of Board -Executive Relations." *Administration in Social Work (19)*(3).

Land, George and Beth Jarman (1992). *Breaking Point and Beyond.* New York: HarperBusiness.

Leavitt, Harold J. (1986). *Corporate Pathfinders.* Homewood, IL: Dow Jones-Irwin.

Leduc, Robert F. and Stephen R Black (1989). "Conjoint Directorship: Clarifying Management Roles Between the Board of Directors and the Executive Director." In Robert D. Herman and Jon Van Til (Editors), Nonprofit Boards of Directors. New Brunswick, NJ: Transaction Publishers.

Legorreta, Judith M and Dennis R. Young (1986). "Why Organizations Turn Nonprofit: Lessons from Case Studies." In Rose-Ackerman, Susan, *The Economics of Nonprofit Institutions* New York: Oxford University Press.

Letts, Christine, William P. Ryan and Allen Grossman (1999). *High Performance Nonprofit Organizations.* New York: John Wiley & Sons.

Liebman, Lance (1984). "Political and Economic Markets: The Public, Private and Not-for-Profit Sectors." In Harvey Brooks, Lance Liebman, and Corinne Schelling (Editors), *Public-Private Partnership.* Cambridge: Ballinger.

Light, Paul C. (1998). Sustaining Innovation: *Creating Nonprofit and Government Organizations That Innovate Naturally.* San Francisco: Jossey-Bass.

Likert, Rensis and Jane G. Likert (1976). *New Ways of Managing Conflict.* New York: McGraw-Hill.

Lipnack, Jessica and Jeffrey Stamps (1993). *The TeamNet Factor.* Essex Junction, VT: Oliver Wright Publications, Inc.

_____ (1982). *Networking: The First and Directory.* Garden City, NY: Doubleday.

Luke, Jeffrey (1998). *Catalytic Leadership.* San Francisco, CA: Jossey-Bass.

Lynn, Lawrence E. (1981). *Managing the Public's Business.* New York: Basic Books.

Mangham, Ian (1979). *The Politics of Organizational Change.* Westport, CT: Greenwood Press.

Mansbridge, Jane (1998). "On the Contested Nature of the Public Good." In Walter W. Powell and Elisabeth S. Clemens (Edited), *Private Action and Public Good.* New Haven: Yale University Press.

_____ (1990, Edited). *Beyond Self-Interest.* Chicago: University of Chicago Press.

Mascotte, John P. (1989). "The Importance of Board Effectiveness in Not-for-Profit Organizations. " In Robert D. Herman and Jon Van Till (Edited), *Nonprofit Boards of Directors.* New Brunswick, NJ; Transaction Publishers.

Mattar, Edward P., II (1985). "The Board in Nonprofit Corporations." In Edward P. Mattar and Michael Ball (Editors), *Handbook for Corporate Directors.* New York: McGraw-Hill.

McFarland, Dalton E. (1986). *The Managerial Imperative.* Cambridge: Ballinger Publishing Company

McLaughlin, Curtis P. (1986). *The Management of Nonprofit Organizations.* New York: John Wiley & Sons.

McLaughlin, Thomas A. (1998). *Nonprofit Mergers & Alliances: A Strategic Planning Guide.* New York: John Wiley & Sons.

McSweeney, Edward (1978). *Managing the Managers.* New York: Harper & Row Publishers.

Middleton, Melissa (1987). "Nonprofit Boards of Directors: Beyond the Governance Function. " In Walter W. Powell (Edited), *The Nonprofit Sector: A Research Handbook.* New Haven: Yale University Press.

Millett, John D. (1980). *Management, Governance and Leadership.* New York AMACOM.

Mintzberg, Henry (1989). *Mintzberg on Management.* New York:
        The Free Press.
_____(1983). *Power In and Around Organizations.* Englewood Cliffs,
        NJ: Prentice-Hall.
Mitroff, I. I. (1983). *Stakeholders of the Organizational Mind.* San
        Francisco: Jossey-Bass Publishers.
Mohrman, A. M. and E. E. Lawler (1985). "The Diffusion of QWL as a
        Paradigm Shift." In W. G. Bennis, K. D. Benne, and R. Chin
        (Editors), *The Planning of Change.* New York: Holt, Rinehart
        and Winston.
Monks, Robert A. and Nell Minow (1991). *Power and Accountability.*
        New York: HarperBusiness.
Morgan, Gareth (1988). *Riding the Waves of Change.* San
        Francisco: Jossey-Bass Publishers.
_____(1986). *Images of Organization.* Beverly Hills, CA: Sage
        Publications.
Mortlock, Mick (2005). "Hurricanes and Learning Organization
        Obsolescence." *The Public Manager* (Fall 2005), 9-12.
Moynihan, Daniel P. (1969). *On Understanding Poverty.* New York:
        Basic Books.
Mueller, Robert K. (1990). *The Director's and Officer's Guide To
        Advisory Boards.* Westport, CT: Quorum Books.
_____ (1986). *Corporate Networking.* New York: The Free Press.
_____ (1984). *Behind the Boardroom Door.* New York: Crown
        Publishers.
_____ (1982).*Board Score.* Lexington, MA: D. C. Heath.
_____ (1981). *The Incompleat Board: The Unfolding of Corporate
        Governance.* Lexington, MA: D. C. Heath.
_____(1979). *Board Compass.* Lexington, MA: D.C. Heath.
_____(1978). *New Directions for Directors.* Lexington, MA:
        D.C.Heath.
_____(1977). *Metadevelopment: Beyond the Bottom Line.* Lexington,
        MA: D. C. Heath.
Murphy, Emmett C. (1994). *Forging the Heroic Organization.*
        Englewood Cliffs, NJ: Prentice Hall.
Musolf, Lloyd D. and Harold Seidman (1980). The Blurred
        Boundaries of Public Administration. " *Public Administration
        Review*, 40:2 (March/April 1980).
Nohria, Nitin and Robert G. Eccles (1992) (Edited). *Networks and
        Organizations: Structure, Form, and Action.* Boston: Harvard
        Business School Press.
Odendahl, Teresa and Elizabeth Boris (1983). "A Delicate Balance:
        Foundation-Board Staff." *Foundation News,* Vol. 24, No. 3.
Odiorne, George S. (1981). *The Change Resisters.* Englewood
        Cliffs, NJ: Prentice-Hall.
_____(1979). *MBO II.* Belmont, CA: Fearon Pitman Publishers.

Ohmae, Kenichi (1982). *The Mind of the Strategist*. New York: McGraw-Hill.

Oleck, Howard L. (1988). *Nonprofit Corporations, Organizations, and Associations* (5th Edition). Englewood Cliffs, NJ: Prentice-Hall.

O'Neil, Michael (1989). *The Third America*. San Francisco: Jossey-Bass Publishers.

Ott, J. Stephen and J. R. Shafritz (1986). *Dictionary of Nonprofit Management*. New York: Fact On File Publications.

Perrow, Charles (1970). "Members as Resources in Voluntary Organizations.' In Rosengren, William R. and Mark Lefton (Editors), *Organizations and Clients*. Columbus, OH: Charles E. Merrill Publishing Company.

Pfeffer, Jeffrey (1987). *Organization Design*. Arlington Heights, IL: AHM Publishing Company.

Pifer, Alan (1967). "The Quasi Nongovernmental Organization." In *Annual Report--1967*, Carnegie Corporation of New York.

Plachy, Roger J. (1987). "Leading vs. Managing: A Guide To Some Critical Distinctions." In A. Dale Timpe, *Leadership*. NY: Fact On File Publications.

Primozic, Kenneth, Edward Primozic, and Joe Leben (1991). *Strategic Choices*. New York: McGraw-Hill.

Ranson, S., B. Hennings, and R. Greenwood (1980). "The Structure of Organizational Futures." *Administrative Science Quarterly*, 25:1.

Redford, Emmette S. (1969). *Democracy and the Administrative State*. New York: Oxford University Press.

Reich, Robert B. (1983). *The Next American Frontier*. New York: Time Books.

Rein, Martin (1989). "The Social Structure of Institutions: Neither Public Nor Private." In Shelia B. Kamerman and Alfred J. Kahn (Editors). *Privatization and the Welfare State*. Princeton: Princeton University Press.

Rudney, Gabriel (1987). "The Scope and Dimensions of Nonprofit Activity." In alter W. Powell (Edited). *The Nonprofit Sector*. New Haven: Yale University Press.

Sagawa, Shirley and Eli Segal (2000). *Common Interest-Common Good: Creating Value through Business and Social Sector Partnerships*. Boston: Harvard Business School Press.

Saidel, Judith R. (1993). "The Board Role in Relation to Government: Alternative Models." In Dennis R. Young, et al., *Governing, Leading, and Managing Nonprofit Organizations*. San Francisco Jossey-Bass Publishers.

Salamon, Lester M. (1995). *Partners in Public Service: Government-Nonprofit Relations in the Modern Welfare State*. Baltimore: Johns Hopkins University Press.

Schon, Donald A. (1971). *Beyond the Stable State.* New York:
    Random House

Schein, Edgar H. (1985). *Organizational Culture and Leadership.*
    San Francisco: Jossey-Bass

Schultze, Charles L. (1977). *The Public Use of Private Interest.* Washington,
    DC: Brookings Institution.

Senge, Peter W. (1990). *The Fifth Dimension.* New York:
    Doubleday/Currency.

Setterberg, Fred and Kary Schulman (1985). *Beyond Profit: The
    Complete Guide To Managing the Nonprofit Organization.*
    New York: Harper and Row.

Shore, Bill (1999). *The Cathedral Within.* New York: Random House

--------(1995). *Revolution of the Heart: A New Strategy for Creating Wealth
    and Meaningful Change.* New York: Riverhead Books.

Simon, Herbert A. (1957). *Administrative Behavior* (2nd Edition).
    New York: Macmillan Company.

Smith, Bruce L. R. (1985). "The Public Use of the Private Sector." In
    Bruce L. R. Smith (Edited). *The New Political Economy.* New
    York: John Wiley and Sons.

Smith, Daniel H. (1980). "The Impact of the Nonprofit Volunteer
    Sector on Society. "In Tracey D. Connors (Edited), *The
    Nonprofit Handbook.* New York: McGraw-Hill.

Smith, David H. and John Dixon (1969). "The Voluntary Society." In
    Edward C. Bursk (Edited), *Challenge To Leadership.* New
    York: Atherton Press.

Stake, R. E. (1979). "Validating Representations: The Evaluator's
    Responsibility." In R. Perloff (edited), *Evaluator
    Interventions: Pros and Cons.* Newbury Park, CA: Sage.

Sumner, Charles E. (1980). *Strategic Behavior in Business and
    Government.* Boston: Little, Brown and Company.

Svendsen, Ann (1998). *The Stakeholder Strategy: Profiting from
    Collaborative Business Relationships.* San Francisco:
    Berrett-Koehler Publishers, Inc.

Taylor, Barbara E., Richard P. Chaiat and Thomas P. Holland (1996).
    The New Work of the Nonprofit Board. Harvard Business
    Review (Sept.-Oct. 1996).

Tichy, Noel M. (1983). *Managing Strategic Change.* New York: John
    Wiley & Sons.

_____ and Mary A. Devanna (1986). *The Transformational Leader.*
    New York: John Wiley and Sons.

Unterman, Israel and Richard H. Davis (1984). *Strategic
    Management for Not-for-Profit Organizations.* New York:
    Praeger.

Ullman, Claire F. (1998). "Partners in Reform: Nonprofit Organizations and the Welfare State in France." In Walter W. Powell and Elisabeth S. Clemens (Edited), *Private Action and the Public Good.* New Haven: Yale University Press

Vail, Peter B. (1989). *Managing as a Performing Art.* San Francisco: Jossey-Bass Publishers.

Waldo, Dwight (1980). *The Enterprise of Public Administration.* Novato, CA: Chandler and Sharp Publishers.

Weidenbaum, Murray (1969). *The Modern Public Sector.* New York: Basic Books.

Weisbrod, Burton A. (1977). *The Voluntary Nonprofit Sector.* Lexington, MA: D.C. Heath.

_____ (1988). *The Nonprofit Economy.* Cambridge: Harvard University Press.

Wheelen, Thomas L. and David Hunger (1987). *Strategic Management* (2nd Edition). Reading, MA: Addison Wesley

White, Michelle J. (1981) (Edited). *Nonprofit Firms in a Three-Sector Economy.* Washington, DC: The Urban Institute.

Widmer, Candice (1989). "Why Board Members Participate." In Robert D. Herman and Jon Van Til (Edited), *Nonprofit Boards of Directors.* New Brunswick: Transaction Publishers.

_____ and Susan Houchin (2000). *The Art of Trusteeship.* San Francisco: Jossey-Bass Publishers.

Wolch, Jennifer R. (1990). *The Shadow State: Government and Voluntary Sector in Transition.* New York: The Foundation Center.

Wolf, Thomas (1990). *Managing a Nonprofit Organization.* New York: Prentice Hall.

Yates, Douglas (1985). *The Politics of Management.* San Francisco: Jossey-Bass Publishers.

Young, Dennis (1983), *If Not for Profit, for What?* Lexington, MA: D. C. Heath

_____ (1986). "Entrepreneurship and the Behavior of Nonprofit Organizations: Elements of a Theory." In Rose-Ackerman, Susan (Ed.), *The Economics of Nonprofit Institutions.* New York: Oxford University Press.

Zald, Mayer N. (1974). "The Power and Functions of Boards of Directors: A Theoretical Synthesis." In Yeheskel Hasenfeld and Richard English (Edited), *Human Service Organizations.* Ann Arbor: University of Michigan Press.

Responsibleness: ethical and moral
 perspectives of, 92; relation to
 "corporate social responsibility" principles, 132
Role, definition of, 9

Sagawa, Shirley, 101-102
Salamon, Lester, 4, 141
Schon, Donald, 114
Schultze, Charles, x(n), 4
SEinvestment^{sTM} and SEinvestors,
 88, 112, 128, 135
Senge, Peter, 40, 122
"Servant leadership," 15
Sibley Hospital, 119
Simon, Herbert, 81-82
Smith, Bruce, x(n)
Social impact, 13; as positive dif-
 ference in people's lives, 15
Social justice, 15, 32, 63
Social welfare, 70
Stake, R. E., 120
Stakeholder analysis, 72 ff
Strategic change, 55
Strategic Governance model: and
 organizational evaluation, 120;
 theory of, xxii-xxiii
Strategies: "same-game" ones, 58;
 "new-game" ones defined, 59
Sumner, Charles, 67
"Sunset" review process, 123

Tinchy, Noel, 55
Triple L Commitments, 41
Trusteeship, defined, 12-13
Two categories of NPS organiza-
 tion markets, 81

ULOC Factor, defined, 18-19
United Methodist Church, IX, XVI,
 27

Values, societal, *passim*
Vendorism, 14, 17
Viability, 111

Vicarious benefits, 90
Vision, 114

Weidenbaum, Murray, x(n)
Wheelen, Thomas, 76
Widmer, Candice, 37
Wolch, Jennifer, x(n), xvii, 5
Wolf, Thomas, 77, 78, 82, 135
Wolfenson, James D., 57-58
Workforce Investment Act, 100

Yates, Douglas, 45

About the Author

W. Astor Kirk has B. A. and M. A. degrees from Howard University and a Ph.D. from the University of Texas. He also has done postgraduate studies at the London School of Economics and Political Science in London, England.

He served as a Regional Director of the U. S. Office of Economic Opportunity (later renamed Community Services Administration) under Presidents Johnson, Nixon, Ford, Carter, and Reagan. He is an adjunct Associate Professor of Organization Theory in the Graduate School of Management and Technology at the University of Maryland; and he has taught at Rutgers University (Camden Campus), Boston University (School of Theology), Howard University, and Huston-Tillotson College.

Head of Organization Management Services Corporation (OMSC), an organization development consulting firm, W. Astor Kirk's consulting assignments include serving as interim chief executive officer of (1) the General Board of Church and Society of the United Methodist Church; (2) the Family Crisis Center of Prince George's County, Maryland; (3) the Hotline & Suicide Prevention Center of Prince George's County; (4) Masthope Mountain Resorts, Inc., a private for-profit resort development firm in the Pennsylvania Pocono's; and (5) Maryland Corporation for Enterprise Development.

Kirk has also served as chairman of the board of trustees of a college and as chairman of the board of directors of many organizations.

He is the author of *DESEGREGATION OF THE METHODIST CHURCH POLITY: Reform Movements that Ended Racial Segregation*, and *NONPROFIT ORGANIZATION GOVERNANCE: A Challenge in Turbulent Times..* Kirk has also written several monographs and articles.

Kirk and his wife Vivian live in Suitland, Maryland.

The author's consulting firm offers seminar and workshop learning experiences for boards of directors and executive managers based on the seven governing roles and responsibilities presented in this book. For information regarding these seminars and workshops, contact the author at:

OMS Company
P. O. Box 470
Suitland, MD 20752
(301) 735-9620
E-mail: Wastork@aol.com